OUR JEWISH ROOTS

Brandon Carpenter

TABLE OF CONTENTS

Forward

"When Paul urged believers to have the 'mind of Messiah' (1 Corinthians 2:16), he wasn't asking them to become Greek philosophers—but Hebraic disciples: people who think covenantally, live obediently, and love relationally."

—Our Jewish Roots

We live in a culture where people will spend hours digging into the backstories of their favorite musicians, actors, or authors. We watch documentaries, follow interviews, and analyze lyrics or performances for hidden meaning—all to gain insight into the person behind the work. In literature classes, we're taught that understanding an author's background helps us interpret their writing more accurately. But when it comes to the Bible—the most influential text in history— most of us are never encouraged to explore the world of its original authors. We're rarely taught to ask, "Who were they? What was their worldview? What cultural and covenantal context shaped their understanding of God?"

Why don't we study Scripture with the same depth and curiosity as we do with any other pursuit?

That's exactly what Brandon Carpenter invites you to do in Our Jewish Roots. This book offers more than historical or theological insight—it offers perspective. Brandon walks you through the foundational aspects of Scripture that are often ignored, misunderstood, or glossed over. These aren't abstract academic ideas. These are deep, transformative truths rooted in the Jewish context of the Bible and the

Messiah—truths that can radically shift how you read God's Word and how you live it out.

I've had the privilege of learning under Brandon's teaching since 2010. At the time, I wasn't looking for anything new. I had been a Christian for 40 years. I was familiar with the stories. When I heard he was teaching from the book of Daniel, I honestly didn't expect to be challenged. I had heard countless sermons on Daniel—what more could there be to learn? But it was Sunday morning, and I needed to choose a class; something nudged me to give it a try.

I'm so glad I did.

That class was a turning point for me. For the first time, I experienced what it meant to have my mind fully engaged in the study of Scripture. Brandon wasn't just teaching facts—he was inviting us into the text. He asked hard questions. He encouraged us to think deeply and challenged us to examine our assumptions. That morning marked the beginning of a journey—a fire for learning (and at times, unlearning and relearning) that has only grown stronger over the years.

I grew up immersed in Christianity. I was educated in Christian schools representing four different denominations. I was deeply involved in church life, attended and led Bible studies, and could quote Scripture with ease. My faith was real, and my knowledge was something I took pride in. But even with all of that, I hadn't seen how much of the Bible I was reading through modern, Western lenses—how much I was missing by not understanding its Hebraic roots.

In 2018, the Carpenters returned to Texas and helped build a new church, and that's when Brandon's teaching became a steady, guiding presence in our community. Having access to his insight week after week has been a gift—one that continues to bless not just me, but our entire congregation. Brandon brings a rare blend of scholarship, clarity, and humility. He draws on years of experience in both public education and ministry, and he knows how to connect with people. He doesn't just talk at you—he walks with you. His goal isn't to impress with knowledge but to equip others to think, study, and grow in faith.

One of the most impactful things Brandon brings to our community is the idea that spiritual maturity is deeply tied to community. He writes:

"Spiritual maturity is measured not only by personal devotion, but by covenantal participation in community life."

That idea has reshaped how I view discipleship. Faith was never meant to be lived in isolation. Yet in modern Christianity, faith is often reduced to a private experience. We're told it's just "me and Jesus," with little regard for tradition, accountability, or shared responsibility. But that's not the model we see in Scripture. Yeshua discipled in community. Paul planted congregations, not just converts. The early believers were deeply rooted in one another's lives, and that context is essential to understanding the Bible rightly.

Brandon's teachings have pushed me—and all of us in our community—to see that truth more clearly. It hasn't always been comfortable. In fact, it has been downright unsettling at times. I've had moments when I've texted my husband a mind-blown emoji in the middle of a teaching session! I have even been mad at times, stretching is no fun at times! Brandon would pose a seemingly simple question, and I'd confidently answer from a place of dogma, only to realize how much I had taken for granted. He has a way of gently exposing those cracks in our foundation—and then helping us rebuild on a stronger foundation.

Change is hard, especially when it means rethinking long-held beliefs. But it's also beautiful. I've seen our community grow more humble, more thoughtful, and more united through this journey. We've become learners again—people hungry for truth, not just a sermon that makes us feel good. I've seen Brandon grow, too, both as a teacher and as a fellow traveler in faith. Our families have become close friends, and I'm honored to be a part of this movement that he's helping to lead.

One of the things I appreciate most about Our Jewish Roots is that it captures the essence of Brandon's teaching style. Each chapter is filled with insight, yes—but also with questions. Real questions. The kind that don't just test your memory, but invite reflection. Don't skip them. Let them challenge you. Let them open your eyes to things you may have never noticed before.

In a world that's increasingly fragmented and uncertain, people are searching for grounding—for identity, for tradition, for connection. And that's exactly what this book offers. As Brandon writes:

"In a postmodern age, where secularism and hyper-individualism reign, the Hebrew mindset offers a grounding alternative. It calls believers back to community, tradition, and concrete action."

This book is a call to rediscover our roots. Not for nostalgia's sake, but for the sake of deeper discipleship and faithfulness.

You may not agree with everything in these pages—and that's okay. Wrestling is part of the process. But I urge you: lean in. Read slowly. Think deeply. Be willing to take off your 21st- century glasses and try to see the Bible as its original writers intended. You'll be amazed at what you discover.

As Brandon reminds us,

"Theology must begin and end in the world of Israel's Scriptures. Only then will we understand the heart of God, the mission of Messiah, and the call of His people."

Maybe this book won't be the catalyst for change you didn't know you needed. But then again— what if it is?

Nita Broadwell

Introduction

The COVID-19 pandemic was a watershed moment for communities around the world. Still, for our Messianic congregation, the lockdowns exposed a deep longing and urgent need to reconnect with the Jewish roots of our faith. Separated from our usual rhythms of worship and fellowship, we found ourselves asking foundational questions—about who we are, where we come from, and what it truly means to follow Yeshua (Jesus) as both Messiah and as a grafted-in part of the people of Israel. This book is the fruit of that season of searching, learning, and rediscovery.

Rediscovering Our Foundations in a Time of Crisis

During the isolation of lockdown, many in our Messianic community realized that our understanding of Scripture, worship, and identity was often filtered through a distinctly Western, sometimes even anti-Jewish, lens. The familiar patterns—Sunday services, sermons, and songs—were suddenly interrupted. We were left with the raw essentials: the Scriptures, our families, and the Jewish calendar that continued to mark time regardless of the world's upheaval. In that stillness, the Spirit stirred a hunger to return to the roots of our faith, to recover the Jewish context of Yeshua and the early *ekklesia* (assembly).

This was not merely an academic pursuit. It was a matter of spiritual survival. The questions that surfaced were not new, but the urgency was: What does it mean to be a Messianic Jew or Gentile? How do we honor the Torah, the feasts, and the traditions of our ancestors while living in the reality of the New Covenant? What is the relationship between the Church and Israel? How do we resist the forces of assimilation and forgetfulness that have, for centuries, sought to sever the Church from its Jewish foundation?

A Sermon Series for a Scattered Congregation

It was in this context—of uncertainty, longing, and spiritual hunger—that I began preparing and delivering a sermon series for our congregation. Though we were physically separated, these teachings became a lifeline for our community, providing structure, hope, and a renewed sense of purpose. Each week, during our virtual and in-person meetings, we explored the Jewish roots of our faith together. The sermons were not just lessons; they were conversations, invitations to wrestle with Scripture and tradition, and opportunities to rediscover our shared identity.

Preaching during this season was unlike any other. The absence of physical gatherings forced me to rethink how to communicate and connect. I found myself drawing more deeply on storytelling, biblical context, and practical application—seeking to make each message not only informative but transformative. The unique needs of our congregation shaped the process: some were new to the Messianic faith, others were lifelong students of Torah, and all were navigating the challenges of a world turned upside down.

The sermon series became a journey, week by week, through the foundational themes of Messianic faith: covenant, identity, feasts, Sabbath, the land and people of Israel, and the ongoing relationship between Jews and Gentiles in Messiah. Each message, though a stand-alone lesson, was built upon the last, weaving together Scripture, history, and personal testimony. The feedback from our community was immediate and heartfelt— people were hungry for this teaching, eager to reclaim what had been lost or forgotten.

When the Church Was Jewish

The earliest followers of Yeshua were, in every sense, Jewish. Their faith was not a departure from Judaism but a fulfillment of Israel's covenantal hope through the Messiah. They lived out their discipleship in the rhythms of Torah, Temple, and synagogue life. Acts 2, often called the "birthday of the Church," was, in fact, a Jewish festival—*Shavu'ot* (Pentecost)—and the outpouring of the Spirit was seen as the promised New Covenant, the Torah written on the heart (Jeremiah 31).

These first believers, known as "Nazarenes" or *HaDerekh* (The Way), continued to keep the Sabbath, observe kosher laws, and celebrate the feasts. They saw themselves as the first fruits of Israel's redemption, not as founders of a new religion. Their faith was communal, rooted in the story of God's covenant with Israel. Even as the early movement spread to Gentiles, the Jewishness of the gospel remained central.

The Tragic Separation and Its Consequences

History, however, tells a story of gradual and then decisive separation. The destruction of the Second Temple, the rise of Rabbinic Judaism, and the influx of Gentile believers into the movement led to increasing tension. By the second century, Messianic Jews found themselves alienated from both the synagogue and the emerging Gentile Church. The Church, eager to define itself in contrast to Judaism, began to distance itself from Jewish customs—replacing Sabbath with Sunday, Passover with Easter, and eventually developing doctrines that rejected the ongoing covenant with Israel.

This separation was not simply theological; it was deeply personal and communal. The addition of prayers like the *Birkat HaMinim*, which cursed "heretics" (often Messianic Jews), made synagogue participation impossible for followers of Yeshua. Meanwhile, the Church's embrace of supersessionism (replacement theology) led to centuries of misunderstanding, persecution, and loss.

The Mosaic Covenant: Grace, Identity, and Community

At the heart of Jewish identity is the Mosaic Covenant—the giving of the Torah at Sinai. Contrary to many Christian misunderstandings, the Torah was not given as a means of earning salvation but as a response to God's prior act of redemption. Israel was redeemed from Egypt first, then given the Torah as a marriage covenant, a *ketubah* defining the responsibilities of love and loyalty.

The Torah is not legalism but grace in action. It is a guide for holy living, a communal calling to embody God's justice, mercy, and holiness. The festivals, the Sabbath, and the commandments shape not only individual piety but the entire life of the community. The presence of God dwells among His people through the rhythms of Torah and Tabernacle.

For Messianic Jews, the Mosaic Covenant remains a living reality. While atonement is found in Yeshua, the Torah continues to shape identity and practice. This is not about earning favor but about responding to God's faithfulness with covenantal love.

Passover: Redemption, Memory, and Messiah

The story of Passover is the heartbeat of Jewish memory and the foundation of the gospel. It is not just a historical event but a living rehearsal of redemption. The blood of the lamb, the unleavened bread, and the journey from slavery to freedom all point to deeper spiritual realities. In the New Covenant, Yeshua is revealed as the ultimate Passover Lamb, whose sacrifice brings liberation from sin and death.

The Passover Seder, with its rituals and symbols, becomes a powerful enactment of the gospel. The *matzah*, the cups of wine, and the retelling of the Exodus story connect us to the past and the hope of final redemption. In celebrating Passover, we remember that salvation is both personal and communal, rooted in the story of Israel and fulfilled in the Messiah.

Sabbath: Covenant of Time and Testimony

Among all the commandments, the Sabbath stands as a unique sign of covenant. It is a weekly declaration that time belongs to God, a sanctuary in time that shapes Jewish identity. For Messianic Jews, the Sabbath is both a remembrance of creation and a testimony to Yeshua, the Lord of the Sabbath.

Sabbath is not a burden but a gift—a taste of the world to come. It is a prophetic witness to the hope of the Messianic Kingdom when all creation will find rest. In a world obsessed with productivity, the Sabbath teaches us to rest, to trust, and to remember who we are.

Israel: People, Land, and Calling

To understand the gospel is to understand Israel—not just as a nation, but as a people with a unique calling. The land of Israel is not merely a political entity but the stage for God's redemptive drama. The election of Israel is not about privilege but about responsibility—to be a light to the nations, a kingdom of priests, and a holy nation.

The tragedy of replacement theology is its erasure of this calling. The New Testament does not replace Israel with the Church; rather, it invites Gentiles to be grafted into the olive tree, sharing in the promises without erasing the distinctiveness of Israel.

Messianic Judaism affirms the ongoing covenant with the Jewish people and the centrality of Israel in God's plan.

One Law for All? Distinction and Unity

A central question for Messianic communities is the relationship between Jews and Gentiles in the Body of Messiah. The Torah speaks of "one law for all" but also makes distinctions between priests, Levites, men, women, and sojourners. The Jerusalem Council (Acts 15) affirmed that Gentiles are welcomed into the covenant community without taking on full Torah obligation. This bilateral ecclesiology[1] preserves both unity and distinction, honoring the diversity of callings within the one Body.

---

[1] Bilateral ecclesiology is an idea developed by Mark Kinzer in his book Post-Missionary Messianic Judaism. It teaches that the Church is made up of two connected groups: Jews and non-Jews (Gentiles). Kinzer says that Jewish people who believe in Jesus should keep their Jewish traditions and identity, while Gentile Christians remain distinct but united with them. This approach respects both the Christian faith and the ongoing importance of Jewish customs, showing that God's promises to the Jewish people continue today. Mark Kinzer is a Messianic Jewish theologian and rabbi who leads this movement.

Jewish Life Cycle and Communal Identity

The Jewish life cycle—birth, circumcision, coming of age, marriage, and death—marks the journey of faith from generation to generation. These rituals are not empty traditions but sacred moments that affirm identity, continuity, and hope. For Messianic Jews, these ceremonies are infused with new meaning in Messiah, proclaiming the faithfulness of God from age to age.

Wrestling with Scripture: A Messianic Approach

Jewish tradition has always embraced the struggle with difficult passages in Scripture. Rather than seeking simplistic answers, we are called to wrestle, to question, and to seek deeper understanding. Messianic Judaism continues this tradition, reading the Scriptures in their Jewish context and seeking the face of God in the midst of ambiguity and tension.

Confronting Anti-Jewish Theology

One of the most painful legacies of Church history is the development of anti-Jewish theology. Supersessionism, the idea that the Church has replaced Israel, led to centuries of misunderstanding, marginalization, and violence. Messianic Judaism stands as a prophetic challenge to this legacy, affirming the irrevocable calling of Israel and the Jewishness of the gospel.

The Atoning Power of the Righteous

At the heart of both Jewish and Messianic thought is the idea that the suffering of the righteous can bring atonement. The sacrificial system, the stories of the martyrs, and the figure of the Suffering Servant in Isaiah 53 all point to this mystery. In Yeshua, the ultimate *tzaddik* (righteous one), we see the fulfillment of this redemptive pattern—a sacrifice not only for Israel but for the nations.

Why This Book? A Call to Return

This book is an invitation to return—not to nostalgia or legalism, but to the living roots of our faith. It is a call to honor the Jewishness of Yeshua, to embrace the fullness of the gospel, and to walk in the rhythms of Torah, Sabbath, and community. It is a plea for reconciliation—between Jew and Gentile, Church and synagogue, past and future.

The COVID-19 lockdowns stripped away our illusions of self-sufficiency and forced us to confront the foundations of our faith. In that crucible, our Messianic community discovered that the only way forward was to look back—to recover the story, the practices, and the hope that sustained Israel through exile, persecution, and renewal.

But most of all, this book is a record of a journey we took together as a congregation. Each chapter is rooted in a sermon delivered during our meeting times, shaped by the questions, prayers, and insights of our community. These messages were not just about information but about transformation—about reclaiming our heritage and living out our calling in a world that desperately needs the light of the Messiah.

May this book serve as a guide for all who seek to understand the Jewish roots of their faith, to heal the wounds of division, and to prepare for the day when all Israel will be saved, and the nations will stream to Jerusalem to learn God's ways. May it inspire a new generation to live as a covenant people, bearing witness to the God who redeems, instructs, and dwells among us.

Let us journey together—Jews and Gentiles, old and young, seekers and sages—as we rediscover our Jewish roots and the fullness of the Messianic hope.

Chapter 1:
When the Church Was Jewish

For a time, the earliest followers of Yeshua were Jewish in every sense—religiously, culturally, and communally. The movement that began in Jerusalem after the resurrection was not a departure from Judaism but a continuation and fulfillment of Israel's covenantal hope through the long-awaited Messiah. This first generation of believers did not imagine themselves as founders of a new religion but rather as participants in the unfolding promises of God to Israel. Their faith in Yeshua was a deeply Jewish experience, lived out in the rhythms of Torah, Temple, and synagogue life.

Pentecost, or *Shavu'ot*, serves as the perfect lens through which to understand this reality. Many Christians have been taught to view the events in Acts 2 as the "birthday of the Church"—as if Pentecost marked the beginning of something entirely new, divorced from what came before. But for the Jewish disciples gathered in Jerusalem on that festival day, it was anything but a rupture. It was, in fact, a prophetic fulfillment.

As the *Ruach ha-Kodesh* (Holy Spirit) was poured out, Peter boldly stood and proclaimed that what they were witnessing had been foretold by the prophet Joel. He quoted, "In the last days… I will pour out My *Ruach* on all flesh…" (Acts 2:17). The crowds that had assembled for *Shavu'ot*, one of the three pilgrimage feasts commanded in Leviticus 23, were devout Jews from every corner of the diaspora. They had come to remember the giving of the Torah at Mount Sinai. According to Jewish tradition, *Shavu'ot* marked the very anniversary of that great covenantal moment.

In this context, the giving of the Spirit was not a departure from Torah but its deepening. Jeremiah 31 had long foretold a New Covenant in which the Torah would be written not just on tablets of stone but on the hearts of God's people. The outpouring of the Spirit was the sign that this promised covenant was being inaugurated. Yeshua had already prepared His disciples for this moment, saying, "You will receive power when the *Ruach ha-Kodesh* has come upon you, and you will be My witnesses in Jerusalem... and to the ends of the earth" (Acts 1:8). Far from breaking with Judaism, the early believers saw themselves as the first fruits of Israel's long-awaited redemption.

These early followers, often called "Nazarenes" or *HaDerekh* (The Way), continued to worship daily in the Temple (Acts 2:46; 3:1; 5:42). They remained active in synagogue life (Acts 9:2; 22:19) and maintained their Jewish identity. They kept the Sabbath, observed kosher dietary laws, and celebrated the feasts. Peter, when confronted with the vision of the sheet in Acts 10, protested, "I have never eaten anything unholy or unclean" (Acts 11:8), showing that his observance was intact.

Sabbath, in particular, held a central place. The Jewish people welcomed the Sabbath like a queen, preparing their homes and hearts for her arrival. After the Sabbath ended, they would gather again for *Havdalah*—a ceremony marking the separation between the sacred and the ordinary. Acts 20:7 records one such meeting: Now on the first day of the week, we gathered to break bread. Paul was talking with

15

them, intending to leave the next day, so he prolonged his speech till midnight. ..." This was a *Motza'ei Shabbat* gathering held Saturday night after the conclusion of the Sabbath. It was not a Sunday morning church service but an extension of the day of rest. As David Stern explains, "The community that gathered on Friday evening as the people of God gathered again on Saturday evening as the body of Messiah."[1]

Even the Catholic Encyclopedia acknowledges that early Christians observed Sunday beginning on Saturday night, consistent with the Jewish reckoning of days from sunset to sunset. Early Church historians agree that these gatherings were held in the evening and were rooted in Jewish Sabbath tradition.[2]

However, history would soon test this early harmony. The First Jewish-Roman War (66–70 CE) brought destruction to Jerusalem and the Second Temple. Roman forces under Vespasian and later Titus crushed the rebellion and decimated the city. Yeshua had warned of this very event: "But when you see Jerusalem surrounded by armies, then recognize that her desolation is near. Then those in Judea must flee to the mountains, and those inside the city must get out, and those in the countryside must not enter her. For these are the days of punishment" (Luke 21:20–22).

The early believers heeded this warning. According to church historian Eusebius, the Messianic Jews fled to Pella,

---

[1] David Stern, *Jewish New Testament Commentary* (Jewish New Testament Publications, 1992).

[2] Catholic Encyclopedia, s.v. "Sunday"; Samuele Bacchiocchi, *From Sabbath to Sunday* (Pontifical Gregorian University Press, 1977).

east of the Jordan River, escaping the devastation. Their survival, while providential, alienated them from the wider Jewish community. While most Jews mourned the loss of the Temple, the Nazarenes did not participate in national mourning. Some rabbis saw this as a betrayal, interpreting the Nazarene's escape as abandonment rather than faithfulness.

In the aftermath of the war, only two major Jewish groups survived: the Pharisees and the Nazarenes. The Pharisees, led by Rabbi Yochanan ben Zakkai, established a new center in Yavne and laid the foundation for what became Rabbinic Judaism. With the Temple gone and the sacrifices ceased, the rabbis emphasized prayer, Torah study, and ethical living as substitutes. This transition was necessary and brilliant, but it also marked a shift away from the diversity of Second Temple Judaism.

For the Nazarenes, however, the destruction of the Temple was not only a tragedy but a validation. Yeshua had declared Himself the ultimate sacrifice, the Lamb of God. His death and resurrection had accomplished what the Temple system foreshadowed. They did not need a rebuilt altar to continue their faith. The final atonement had already been made.

The tension between Rabbinic leaders and the Nazarenes intensified. Around 90 CE, the *Birkat HaMinim* was added to the Amidah (The Standing Prayer - Eighteen Benedictions). This prayer cursed the heretics—initially a general category but increasingly aimed at Messianic Jews. It read, "May the minim perish in an instant; may they be blotted out of the book of life."[3]

With this addition, the Messianic community could no longer participate in synagogue worship without cursing themselves. This was not simply a theological debate but a community exclusion. Those who confessed Yeshua as Messiah were excommunicated from Jewish life.

Rabbinic literature tells stories that reflect this growing divide. One tale recounts Hanina, the nephew of Rabbi Joshua ben Hananiah, who was exiled after embracing the gospel. Another tells of Eleazer ben Dama, who was bitten by a snake and sought healing from Jacob, a Nazarene healer. Rabbi Ishmael refused, insisting it was better for him to die than be healed by a follower of Yeshua.[4] These narratives, while polemical, reveal the deep mistrust that had taken root.

By the early second century, the division was clear. Messianic Jews were viewed with suspicion by both the emerging Church and Rabbinic Judaism. To the rabbis, they were traitors; to the Gentile believers flooding into the movement, they were anomalies. As the Church became increasingly Gentile, it began to distance itself from Jewish customs. Sunday worship replaced the Sabbath. Easter replaced Passover. The Church began to define itself not in continuity with Israel but in contrast to it.

This shift was not inevitable, nor was it faithful to the apostles' vision. Paul had warned Gentile believers not to boast against the natural branches (Romans 11:18). He

---

[3] Birkat HaMinim, 12th benediction of the Amidah.
[4] Tosefta Hullin 2:22–24.

envisioned a unified *ekklesia* made up of Jews and Gentiles, distinct yet interdependent. "For if their rejection leads to the reconciliation of the world, what will their acceptance be but life from the dead" (Romans 11:15).

The early Church's Jewishness is not a mere historical curiosity. It is a vital key to understanding the gospel, the Scriptures, and God's unfolding plan. Recovering this heritage is a prophetic act of reconciliation, an answer to the prayer of Yeshua: "that they all may be one" (John 17:21).

Today, Messianic Jewish communities around the world are seeking to restore what was lost—not as a nostalgia project, but as a foretaste of the age to come. The fullness of the *ekklesia* requires both Jew and Gentile to walk together in mutual respect, covenantal love, and shared mission.

Reflection Questions:

- How does understanding the Jewish context of Acts 2 reshape your view of Pentecost?

- Why did the early followers of Yeshua continue Temple and synagogue worship?

- What social and political forces led to the exclusion of Messianic Jews from Jewish life?

- In what ways has the modern Church misunderstood or neglected its Jewish roots?

- How can restoring the Jewishness of the gospel impact Jewish-Christian relations today?

Chapter 2:
The Mosaic Covenant – Torah, Identity, and Covenant Faithfulness

The Mosaic Covenant occupies a central place in the biblical narrative. It is at Mount Sinai that the children of Israel receive the Torah and are publicly identified as a nation set apart for divine purposes. This covenant, though often misunderstood or dismissed within Christian theology as a temporary legal system, is the bedrock of Jewish identity and a vital component in the unfolding drama of redemption. Far from being opposed to grace or superseded by the New Covenant, the Mosaic Covenant reveals the relational and ethical nature of God and calls Israel to embody His holiness among the nations.

Sinai: A Marriage Covenant

The imagery used in Exodus 19–24 is that of a betrothal. God, having redeemed Israel from bondage in Egypt, brings His people to Mount Sinai and proposes a covenant relationship: "Now then, if you listen closely to My voice and keep My covenant, then you will be My own treasure from among all people, for all the earth is Mine. So as for you, you will be to Me a kingdom of kohanim and a holy nation" (Exodus 19:5-6). The language echoes ancient Near Eastern suzerainty treaties, but the relational intimacy goes beyond contract—it is the language of marital fidelity.

When the people respond, "All that Adonai has spoken we will do," they are saying "I do" to this covenantal union (Exodus 19:8). The giving of the Torah is not a burdensome law code but a *ketubah*—a covenantal document defining the responsibilities of love, loyalty, and mutual commitment.

Torah as Grace, Not Legalism

A common misconception in Christian theology is that the Torah was given as a means of earning salvation. Yet this stands in direct contradiction to the narrative sequence of Exodus. Israel is redeemed first—delivered from Egypt by God's mighty hand—and only afterward brought to Sinai to receive the Torah for the purpose of instruction. Redemption precedes obligation. Grace is the foundation of the covenant.

Jewish thought has long held that Torah is not a burden but a gift. The rabbis teach that the Torah existed before creation, and that God looked into the Torah to create the world.[1] The psalmist declares, "Oh, how I love Your Torah! It is my meditation all day" (Psalm 119:97). Paul himself affirms the goodness of the Torah: "So then, the Torah is holy, and the commandment is holy and righteous and good" (Romans 7:12).

In this sense, Torah becomes a guide for holy living—a means by which the redeemed people of God express their identity and mission. It is not legalism, but covenantal responsiveness.

A National and Communal Calling

Unlike the personal relationship emphasized in later evangelical frameworks, the Mosaic Covenant is profoundly communal. God does not call individuals at Sinai but a people: "So as for you, you will be to Me a kingdom of *kohanim* and a

---

[1] Genesis Rabbah 1:1

holy nation" (Exodus 19:6). This corporate identity forms the basis for Israel's mission among the nations.

The commandments given at Sinai are thus not arbitrary rules but expressions of justice, mercy, and holiness. They govern not only personal behavior but societal structures: care for the poor, fair treatment of foreigners, ethical business practices, environmental stewardship, and the administration of justice.

Moreover, the festivals of Leviticus 23 embed Israel's calendar in a rhythm of sacred time—*Shabbat* (Sabbath), *Pesach* (Passover), *Shavuot* (Pentecost), *Yom Kippur* (Day of Atonement), *Sukkot* (Feast of Booths) —inviting continual remembrance of God's redemptive acts and anticipation of His future interventions.

Torah and the Presence of God

The Mosaic Covenant is not merely about laws; it is about hosting the presence of God. The instructions for the Tabernacle (Exodus 25–40) come immediately after the covenant is ratified. God desires to dwell among His people: "Have them make a Sanctuary for Me, so that I may dwell among them" (Exodus 25:8).

This covenant presence is later carried into the Land, and eventually into the Temple in Jerusalem. The Torah and the Tabernacle go hand-in-hand—God's law and God's presence are inseparable.

The Golden Calf and Covenant Renewal

Despite the glorious encounter at Sinai, Israel quickly falls into idolatry. The sin of the golden calf (Exodus 32) is a violation not merely of a command but of covenantal fidelity. Yet in a powerful display of mercy, God renews the covenant. Moses ascends Sinai again, receives the second tablets, and the covenant is re-established.

This moment foreshadows the pattern of exile and return, sin and restoration, that will characterize Israel's history. It also testifies to the enduring nature of the Mosaic Covenant—even in failure, there is forgiveness and the possibility of renewal.

Mosaic Covenant and the New Covenant

In Christian theology, the Mosaic Covenant is often juxtaposed with the New Covenant, as if the former is obsolete and the latter replaces it. But this dichotomy misrepresents the continuity of Scripture. Jeremiah 31:31-34 speaks of a New Covenant in which the Torah will be written on the heart. This is not a cancellation of the Mosaic Covenant but its internalization.

Yeshua affirms this in the Sermon on the Mount: "Do not think that I came to abolish the Torah or the Prophets! I did not come to abolish, but to fulfill" (Matthew 5:17). His teaching intensifies the demands of Torah by moving them from external compliance to internal transformation.

The writer of Hebrews affirms that the Mosaic system was a shadow pointing to the substance—Messiah (Hebrews 10:1). But the shadow is not evil. Rather, it is preparatory and prophetic. Yeshua, the ultimate High Priest, fulfills the sacrificial system by offering Himself once for all. Yet the ethical, communal, and spiritual values embedded in the Mosaic Covenant remain vital.

Messianic Jewish Identity and Torah

For Messianic Jews, the Mosaic Covenant continues to shape identity and practice. While atonement is found in Yeshua, the Torah remains a living expression of covenant life. This distinguishes Messianic Judaism from both mainstream Christianity and non- Messianic Judaism. It affirms the enduring covenant between God and Israel while also recognizing the redemptive fulfillment found in Yeshua.

Paul captures this dynamic in Romans 9:4-5, where he affirms that to Israel belong "the adoption, the glory, the covenants, the giving of the Torah, the Temple service, and the promises." These gifts are not revoked but remain operative in God's plan.

Conclusion: Covenant as Calling

The Mosaic Covenant is not a relic of the past, but a present calling. It summons Israel to be a light to the nations, a people marked by justice, compassion, and holiness. For Messianic believers, it serves as a bridge, anchoring faith in the rich soil of Jewish tradition while proclaiming Yeshua as the fulfillment of God's promises.

Far from being replaced, the covenant at Sinai continues to speak. Its voice echoes in the teachings of Yeshua, the letters of Paul, and the life of the Messianic community. It reminds us that salvation is not merely about individual destiny but communal vocation. It is a call to live as a covenant people, bearing witness to the God who redeems, instructs, and dwells among us.

<u>Reflection and Discussion Questions:</u>

- How does viewing the Torah as a marriage covenant change our understanding of its purpose?

- Why is it significant that Israel was redeemed before receiving the Torah?

- In what ways is the Mosaic Covenant communal rather than individual?

- How does the Mosaic Covenant prepare the way for the New Covenant?

- What is the relevance of Torah for Messianic Jews today?

Chapter 3:
The Meaning of Passover –
Redemption, Memory, and Messiah

Passover (*Pesach*) is not merely a historical remembrance of Israel's deliverance from Egypt. It is a multilayered celebration of redemption that speaks to identity, purpose, and eschatological hope. The story of the Exodus is the heartbeat of Jewish memory, but it is also the foundation of the gospel. In the Passover narrative, we encounter the character of God as redeemer, the nature of the covenant, and the foreshadowing of the Messiah. For Messianic Jews, Passover becomes the stage upon which the drama of salvation is reenacted—not just in memory of the past but as a celebration of its ultimate fulfillment in Yeshua.

The Historical Event: God Redeems

The story of the Exodus begins with oppression. The Israelites, enslaved for centuries in Egypt, cry out, and God hears their groaning (Exodus 2:23-25). The divine response to suffering is not silence but action. God raises up Moses as a deliverer and confronts Pharaoh with the demand to release His people.

Each plague demonstrates God's authority over the false gods of Egypt. The climax comes with the tenth plague—the death of the firstborn. Only those who mark their doorposts with the blood of the lamb are spared. This blood is not magical but covenantal. It is the sign of obedience and trust. "When I see the blood, I will pass over you. So there will be no plague among you to destroy you when I strike the land of Egypt" (Exodus 12:13).

The Hebrew word *Pesach* means "to pass over" or "to protect." The blood-covered homes are shielded by divine mercy. This event is not only deliverance from physical bondage but the beginning of a new identity. Israel becomes a nation through this act of redemption.

The Feast: Memory as Identity

God commands that this event be remembered yearly: "Also you are to observe this event as an eternal ordinance, for you and your children." (Exodus 12:24). Passover is not a one-time celebration. It becomes a rehearsal of redemption—every generation must see themselves as if they had personally come out of Egypt.[1]

This emphasis on memory is foundational in Jewish life. Memory is not passive recall but active identity formation. When Jews retell the Exodus at the Passover Seder, they are not merely recounting history—they are embodying the covenant story. This is the foundation of Jewish peoplehood: a collective memory of divine rescue and calling.

The *Haggadah* (the telling of the story), read at the Seder, leads the participants through this story, invoking Scripture, song, and ritual. From the four cups of wine to the *afikomen* (the broken piece of bread that was wrapped up and hidden for a time during the meal), every element of the Seder draws the participant into the redemptive journey.

The Lamb: A Foreshadowing of Messiah

The central figure in the original Passover was the lamb. It had to be without blemish, its bones were not to be broken

---

[1] Mishnah Pesachim 10:5.

(Exodus 12:46), and it was to be consumed in haste. This lamb became the substitute for the household, their firstborn spared because of its sacrifice.

In the New Testament, Yeshua is clearly identified with the Passover lamb. John the Immerser declares, "Behold, the Lamb of God who takes away the sin of the world" (John 1:29). Paul writes, "Messiah, our Passover Lamb, has been sacrificed" (1 Corinthians 5:7).

The parallels are striking Yeshua enters Jerusalem during the time of lamb selection; He is without blemish, examined and found faultless (Luke 23:4); His bones are not broken (John 19:36); and His blood becomes the covering for those who trust in Him.

The timing of His death during Passover is not accidental—it is theological. Just as the original lamb marked the beginning of Israel's redemption, Yeshua's sacrifice inaugurates the new covenant and delivers us from the slavery of sin.

The Seder and the Last Supper

Yeshua's last meal with His disciples was a Passover Seder (Luke 22:15). Within that familiar setting, He reinterprets elements of the meal in light of His impending death. Taking the unleavened bread (*matzah*), He says, "This is My body, given for you." Taking the third cup—the cup of redemption—He says, "This cup is the new covenant in My blood" (Luke 22:19-20).

This was not a repudiation of Passover but its deep fulfillment. The Exodus story pointed forward to a greater liberation. As the physical redemption from Egypt required the blood of the lamb, so too does the spiritual redemption of all humanity require the blood of the Messiah.

The *matzah*, pierced and striped, becomes a visible symbol of Yeshua's suffering. The *afikomen*—the bread that was broken, hidden, and then returned—is a powerful image of His death, burial, and resurrection. In Messianic Seders today, these symbols come alive with renewed meaning.

Leaven, Repentance, and Sanctification

In preparation for Passover, Jewish households search for and remove all *chametz* (leaven). Leaven represents sin, arrogance, and corruption. Paul alludes to this when he writes, "Let us celebrate the feast not with old *chametz*… but with unleavened bread—the *matzah* of sincerity and truth" (1 Corinthians 5:8).

Removing leaven becomes an act of spiritual cleansing. It is a call to repentance, a turning away from the old life of bondage. This theme resonates with Paul's teaching that "A little *hametz* works its way through the whole batch of dough" (Galatians 5:9).

Thus, Passover is a time of renewal. It challenges believers to leave behind the Egypt of sin and to walk in the freedom of new life. Just as Israel was redeemed to serve God, so too are we redeemed to live in holiness and truth.

The Eschatological Hope: The Final Redemption

Passover not only looks back but looks forward. The Seder ends with the words "Next year in Jerusalem!"—a declaration of hope for the Messianic Age. The deliverance from Egypt is a type of the greater redemption to come.

In Jewish eschatology, the Messiah is seen as the one who will bring the final exodus. Just as Moses led Israel out of Egypt, so the Messiah will lead all nations into the Kingdom of God. Isaiah 11 and Ezekiel 36 envision a future where God gathers His people, restores the land, and fills the earth with His glory For Messianic believers, this hope is anchored in Yeshua's resurrection and His promise to return. Just as the first Passover led to Mount Sinai, so our redemption leads us toward the New Jerusalem.

Conclusion: Passover and the Gospel

Passover is not a relic of the past but a living revelation. It calls us to remember that we were slaves—and that God intervened. It reminds us that redemption requires sacrifice, that freedom is for holiness, and that God is faithful to His covenant.

In Yeshua, the deeper meaning of Passover is revealed. He is the Lamb who was slain, the Redeemer who leads us out, the Bread who sustains us, and the Lord who will come again. Celebrating Passover as followers of Messiah is not an appropriation of Jewish tradition—it is a return to the roots of our faith. It is a declaration that the gospel is Jewish, that salvation is from the Jews (John 4:22) and that the story of Israel is the story of redemption for the whole world.

<u>Reflection and Discussion Questions:</u>

- How does understanding Passover enrich your understanding of Yeshua's death and resurrection?

- What are the spiritual parallels between the Exodus from Egypt and personal salvation?

- Why is it significant that Yeshua chose Passover to reveal the New Covenant?

- In what ways can believers today embody the message of Passover in their lives?

- What hope does the Passover story offer for the future Messianic Kingdom?

Chapter 4:
The Sabbath and the Jew – A Covenant of Time and Testimony

Among all the commandments given to Israel, none stands out more clearly as a sign of the covenant than the Sabbath (*Shabbat*). *Shabbat* is not simply a day of rest—it is a weekly reenactment of God's creative sovereignty and redemptive power. For Jews, Sabbath observance has always functioned as a marker of identity, a sanctification of time, and a testimony to the world. For Messianic Jews, it becomes a double testimony: to the God of creation and Yeshua, the Lord of the Sabbath.

Sabbath as Creation and Covenant

The roots of the Sabbath lie in Genesis. "God completed—on the seventh day—His work that He made, and He ceased—on the seventh day—from all His work that He made. Then God blessed the seventh day and sanctified it, for on it He ceased from all His work that God created for the purpose of preparing" (Genesis 2:2 3). The first thing God declares holy is not a place or an object, but time. From the beginning, the Sabbath is woven into the fabric of creation.

When Israel receives the command at Sinai, it is framed not only as a day of rest, but as a sign: "Surely you must keep My *Shabbatot*, for it is a sign between Me and you throughout your generations, so you may know that I am *ADONAI* who sanctifies you" (Exodus 31:13). Sabbath is not merely practical—it is deeply theological. It declares that

33

time belongs to God and that Israel is His set-apart people.

Rabbinic tradition calls the Sabbath a "taste of the world to come" (*Olam HaBa*), a weekly moment when the peace of Messianic fulfillment breaks into the present[1] In this way, Sabbath becomes both a sign and a promise.

The Experience of the Jew: More Than a Day Off

For observant Jews throughout the centuries, the Sabbath has not been a restriction but a liberation. It is a holy time when the soul can rest and reconnect with God, family, and community. Abraham Joshua Heschel famously called it a "cathedral in time"—a sanctuary not built with hands but sanctified through obedience.[2]

The traditional Friday night *Kabbalat Shabbat* service welcomes the Sabbath like a bride. The lighting of candles, the singing of *L'cha Dodi*, the blessing of children, and the festive meal all embody joy and reverence. It is a celebration of the God who both created the universe and redeemed Israel from Egypt (Deuteronomy 5:15).

Jewish law (*halakhah*) lays out 39 categories of forbidden labor, not to oppress, but to protect the sacredness of rest. To cease from work is to declare, "I am not defined by my productivity but by my relationship with God."

Yeshua and the Sabbath

For many Christians, Yeshua's actions on the Sabbath appear as violations of the Torah. Yet in every case, He clarifies the true intent of the Sabbath: restoration, mercy,

---

[1] Babylonian Talmud, Berakhot 57b.
[2] Abraham Joshua Heschel, *The Sabbath* (New York: Farrar, Straus and Giroux, 1951).

and life. "Then He said to them, "*Shabbat* was made for man, and not man for *Shabbat*." He said, "So the Son of Man is Lord even of *Shabbat*" (Mark 2:27 28).

Yeshua heals on the Sabbath—not to reject Torah but to fulfill it. In Luke 13:10–17, He heals a woman bent over for eighteen years, saying, "So this one, a daughter of Abraham incapacitated by satan for eighteen years, shouldn't she be set free from this imprisonment on *Yom Shabbat*?" In doing so, He shows that Sabbath is not about rigid rule-keeping but about covenantal wholeness.

He attended synagogue regularly on the Sabbath (Luke 4:16), honored its rhythms, and never instructed His disciples to abandon it. Rather, He embodied its deepest meaning—restoration and redemption. The Sabbath miracles of Yeshua were not violations but revelations.

The Early Messianic Believers and the Sabbath

The first followers of Yeshua were Sabbath-keepers. Acts records that Paul and other apostles taught in synagogues on *Shabbat* (Acts 13:14–44; 17:2). There was no sense that the Sabbath had been abolished. Rather, it continued as the communal rhythm of Jewish believers.

Some of the confusion comes from Acts 20:7, where believers gathered "on the first day of the week." But this refers to *Motza'ei Shabbat*—Saturday night after Sabbath had ended—when the early believers came together for teaching and fellowship. This was not a transfer of Sabbath to Sunday, but a continuation of communal gathering

Historical sources such as the *Didache* and early church fathers confirm that Jewish believers kept the Sabbath, while

Gentile believers met on Sunday. The division came not from apostolic teaching, but from later efforts to distinguish Christianity from Judaism, especially after the *Bar Kokhba* revolt.

Constantine and the Shift to Sunday

In the early fourth century, Emperor Constantine legalized Christianity and sought to unify his empire under one religious expression. In 321 CE, he issued a decree mandating rest on "the venerable day of the sun"—Sunday. This was not a theological move but a political one. It aligned Christianity with Roman solar worship and distanced it from Jewish customs.[3]

By the Council of Laodicea (c. 363 CE), Sunday observance was codified, and Sabbath- keeping was explicitly forbidden to Christians: "Christians must not Judaize by resting on the Sabbath, but must work on that day."[4] This marks the official beginning of Sabbath's erasure from Christian life.

Yet, throughout history, remnants of Sabbath observance remained among Eastern Christians, Ethiopian believers, and medieval sects. Today, many Messianic Jews and some Gentile Christians are recovering the biblical Sabbath, not as legalism but as love.

The Sabbath as Prophetic Witness

Sabbath is more than a memorial—it is a prophecy. Hebrews 4:9 declares, "So there remains a *Shabbat* rest for the people of God." The Sabbath points to the final rest in the

---

[3] Codex Theodosianus 2.8.1 (321 CE).
[4] Council of Laodicea, Canon 29.

Messianic Kingdom when creation will be restored and all will dwell in peace.

Isaiah envisions this day: "from one *Shabbat* to another, all flesh will come to bow down before Me," says *ADONAI*" (Isaiah 66:23). The Sabbath is not limited to Sinai—it is rooted in Eden and stretches into eternity.

For this reason, Sabbath is a spiritual discipline that forms us into people of hope. It is a weekly resistance to the culture of busyness. It trains us to live as though the Kingdom has already come.

Messianic Jewish Practice Today

For Messianic Jews, keeping the Sabbath is not an attempt to earn righteousness but a joyful expression of identity. It is a connection of their ancestors and their Messiah. In our communities, *Shabbat* is welcomed with songs and candles, Torah reading and blessings, *challah* (braided bread) and wine.

Messianic congregations often hold *Erev Shabbat* services on Friday evening and Torah services on Saturday morning. It is a time of worship, fellowship, teaching, and joy. The Sabbath becomes a witness—first to the Jewish people, and then to the world—that the God of Israel is faithful.

Some Gentile believers join in Sabbath observance, not to become Jews, but to embrace the richness of God's appointed times. This can be done with sensitivity and honor, recognizing the distinct calling of Israel and the unity of the Body of Messiah.

Conclusion: Sabbath as Resistance and Rest

In a world of relentless striving, the Sabbath offers a holy pause. It reminds us that our worth is not in what we do but in who we are. It is the weekly declaration that God reigns, that time is sacred, and that redemption is real.

For the Jew, the Sabbath is a covenant sign. For the Messianic Jew, it is also a sign of the Messiah who brings ultimate rest. For the Gentile believer, it is an invitation to taste the goodness of God's rhythm. In every case, the Sabbath is a gift—a testimony to creation, redemption, and the hope of new creation.

As the writer of Hebrews exhorts, let us strive to enter that rest—not only in the world to come but each week, as we remember and rejoice in the God who sanctifies time.

Reflection and Discussion Questions:

- How does the Sabbath function as a sign of covenant for the Jewish people?

- What did Yeshua's Sabbath healings reveal about the heart of God?

- Why did early Jewish believers continue to observe Shabbat?

- How did political and theological shifts lead to Sunday observance?

- What does Sabbath observance look like in Messianic communities today?

Chapter 5:
The Meaning of Israel – People, Land, and Calling

Israel. The name evokes passion, controversy, and promise. For some, it is a geopolitical reality; for others, a symbol of spiritual continuity. Yet within the biblical narrative and Jewish tradition, Israel is not simply a country—it is a calling, a covenantal identity, and a people uniquely chosen to reflect the holiness of God. In Messianic Judaism, understanding the meaning of Israel is essential not only to Jewish identity but also to the integrity of the gospel.

Israel as a Chosen People

The first mention of "Israel" occurs when Jacob wrestles with the angel and receives a new name: "Your name will no longer be Jacob, but rather Israel, for you have struggled with God and with men, and you have overcome" (Genesis 32:28). From this moment, Israel becomes both a person and a people. The children of Israel are the physical descendants of Jacob, and through them God will reveal His redemptive purposes.

God's election of Israel is not rooted in their greatness but in His covenantal love.

"It is not because you are more numerous than all the peoples that *ADONAI* set His love on you and chose you— for you are the least of all peoples. Rather, because of His love for you and His keeping the oath He swore to your fathers, *ADONAI* brought you out with a mighty hand and redeemed you from the house of slavery, from the hand of Pharaoh king of Egypt" (Deuteronomy 7:7–8). This divine choosing is for service: to be a "kingdom of *kohanim* and a holy nation" (Exodus 19:6), a light to the nations (Isaiah 42:6).

Rabbinic sources echo this vocational identity. The *Sifre* on Deuteronomy explains that Israel's chosenness comes with obligation—to study Torah, to walk in God's ways, and to sanctify His name.[1] Election is not about privilege; it is about responsibility.

The Land of Israel – Covenant and Holiness

The covenant with Abraham includes not only descendants but land: "I give this land to your seed" (Genesis 15:18). The land of Israel is not arbitrary. It is the stage upon which the divine drama unfolds. It is the place of promise, of testing, and of return.

The holiness of the land is contingent upon obedience. The Torah repeatedly warns that the land will "vomit out" its inhabitants if they defile it (Leviticus 18:28). The exile of Israel is not merely political—it is theological. The land itself is a partner in the covenant.

Jewish prayers have always included the hope of return. The Amidah petitions God to "gather us in from the four corners of the earth."[2] The Passover Seder ends with "Next year in Jerusalem!" These longings were not metaphorical. They were rooted in the tangible hope of restoration.

Modern Zionism, while political in form, echoes these

---

[1] Sifre Devarim 343.
[2] Amidah, Blessing 10.

ancient aspirations. The return to the land in the 20th century was not the fulfillment of all prophecy, but it was undeniably a significant stage in the unfolding of Israel's redemptive story.

Israel and the Messiah

Within the Jewish tradition, the Messiah is the one who restores Israel—not only spiritually, but nationally. Rambam (Maimonides) writes that the Messiah will "gather the dispersed of Israel," rebuild the Temple, and reestablish Torah law.[3] This vision ties the destiny of Israel to the identity of the Messiah.

In the New Testament, Yeshua is portrayed not as an outsider to Israel but as its fulfillment. He is born of Jewish lineage (Matthew 1), lives as a Torah-observant Jew, and declares that He has come "only to the lost sheep of the house of Israel" (Matthew 15:24). His ministry affirms the promises to the patriarchs while also opening the door for Gentiles to be grafted into the covenant (Romans 11).

Paul's vision is not a replacement of Israel but a reconciliation of Israel and the nations. "I say then, God has not rejected His people, has He? May it never be!" (Romans 11:1). The olive tree remains Israel; Gentile believers are wild branches grafted in. The root remains Jewish.

The Tragedy of Replacement Theology

Throughout much of Christian history, the church taught that it had replaced Israel in God's plan. This theology, known as supersessionism, claimed that the Jewish people were no longer the chosen people. Their rejection of

---

[3] Maimonides, *Mishneh Torah*, Hilchot Melachim 11.

Messiah, it was argued, disqualified them from the covenant.

This doctrine led to centuries of anti-Judaism, persecution, and theological distortion. It severed the church from its roots and distorted the meaning of both Old and New Covenants. It replaced the particularity of Israel with a vague universalism and stripped the gospel of its Jewish context.

Messianic Judaism stands as a challenge to this theology. It proclaims that God's promises to Israel are irrevocable (Romans 11:29), and that Yeshua has not nullified the covenant but confirmed it. The existence of Jewish followers of Yeshua is itself a testimony to God's faithfulness.

Israel and the Nations – A Bilateral Covenant

One of the foundational insights of Messianic Jewish theology is bilateral ecclesiology—the idea that Jews and Gentiles are both part of the Body of Messiah but with distinct covenantal identities. This is not division; it is distinction.

In Acts 15, the Jerusalem Council does not require Gentiles to take on full Torah observance. Instead, they are given four minimal standards, rooted in Leviticus 17–18. This reflects the ancient Noachide expectations for the nations. The implication is clear:

Jews remain obligated to Torah as a sign of their covenant, while Gentiles are welcomed into fellowship without erasing their identity.

This model honors both continuity and inclusion. It allows Israel to remain Israel, while welcoming the nations into partnership. It reflects the prophetic vision of Zechariah:

"Ten men from the nations… will seize the *tzitzit* of a Jew and say, 'Let us go with you, for we have heard God is with you'" (Zechariah 8:23).

Israel's Calling in the World to Come

The final chapters of Scripture point toward a restored Israel in a restored world. Revelation speaks of the twelve tribes, the New Jerusalem, and the Lamb enthroned. The Messianic Age is not the erasure of Israel but its glorification. "For *Torah* will go forth from Zion and the word of *ADONAI* from Jerusalem" (Isaiah 2:2–4).

The Jewish people are not simply a conduit of past revelation—they are central to God's future plan. The return of Messiah is linked to the repentance of Israel (Matthew 23:39). The resurrection of Israel is the key to the resurrection of the world.

Conclusion: The Mystery of Israel

Israel is a mystery—beloved yet often estranged, chosen yet still waiting, called yet still journeying. But this mystery is at the heart of God's redemptive plan. To understand the gospel is to understand Israel—not as a relic of the past, but as the foundation of the future.

As Messianic believers, we affirm the ongoing calling of the Jewish people, the centrality of the land, and the fulfillment of promise in Yeshua. We reject all forms of replacement and reaffirm the covenant faithfulness of God.

To love the God of Israel is to love the people of Israel. And to walk with the Messiah of Israel is to walk in hope that one day, "all Israel will be saved" (Romans 11:26).

Reflection and Discussion Questions:

- What does it mean that Israel is both a people and a calling?

- How does the land of Israel function within the covenant?

- In what ways did Yeshua affirm and fulfill the promises made to Israel?

- Why is replacement theology both theologically and ethically problematic?

- How can bilateral ecclesiology foster unity while preserving distinct callings?

Chapter 6:
One Law for All? A Messianic Understanding of Distinctions in Torah

The question of whether there is "one law for all" or a distinction between Jewish and Gentile believers in relation to Torah is one of the most debated issues within Messianic Judaism. At the heart of the discussion is the desire to be faithful to Scripture, to honor God's covenantal order, and to understand the diverse roles within the unified Body of Messiah. This chapter explores the meaning of the phrase "one law for all" in context, the difference between covenant and commandment, and how Jewish and Gentile believers share in the promises of God without erasing divinely ordained distinctions.

The Phrase "One Law for All" in Context

The phrase "one law for all" originates from several passages in the Torah, most notably Numbers 15:15–16: "The community will have the same rule for you as well as for the resident outsider. It will be a lasting statute throughout your generations. As for you, so for the outsider will it be before *ADONAI*. The same *Torah* and the same regulations will apply to both you and the outsider residing among you." At first glance, this seems to suggest uniform Torah obligation for both Jews and Gentiles. However, context is key.

These passages typically appear in reference to specific

cases—sacrifices, Passover observance, or judicial matters within Israel. They do not imply a blanket obligation for every commandment but rather affirm that foreigners who *join themselves* to Israel in worship and sacrificial participation must do so respectfully, under the same standards as Israelites.[1]

Rabbinic tradition affirms this balance. The Talmud makes a clear distinction between the obligations of Jews and those of Gentile "God-fearers" or righteous among the nations.[2] The Noahide laws—seven universal laws given to all humanity—were understood as the foundational expectations for Gentiles. Full Torah obligation was only taken on through conversion to Judaism.

Israel's Distinct Calling

Torah was given to Israel as a national constitution. As Psalm 147:19–20 states, "He declares His word to Jacob, His decrees and His rulings to Israel. He has not done so with any other nation. They have not known His judgments. *Halleluyah!*" Israel's election involved the giving of Torah, the priesthood, the Temple, and the land. The *mitzvot* (commandments) are not merely spiritual ethics—they are cultural, covenantal, and national identifiers.

Messianic Jewish theologian Mark Kinzer affirms that Torah observance remains a valid expression of Jewish identity in Messiah.[3] Yeshua did not nullify Jewish covenantal life; rather, He fulfilled its deepest purpose. He

---

[1] Exodus 12:48–49; Leviticus 17:8–9.
[2] Babylonian Talmud, Sanhedrin 56a.
[3] Mark Kinzer, Postmissionary Messianic Judaism (Grand Rapids: Brazos Press, 2005).

declared, "I tell you, until heaven and earth pass away, not the smallest letter or serif[c] shall ever pass away from the *Torah* until all things come to pass" (Matthew 5:17–19).

For Gentiles, inclusion in the covenant community does not necessitate becoming Jews. Paul uses the analogy of grafting in wild branches (Romans 11). Gentiles are brought near to the covenants (Ephesians 2:12–13), not by adopting every aspect of Jewish Torah observance, but by trusting in the Messiah of Israel and being filled with the Spirit.

The Jerusalem Council and Distinct Responsibilities

Acts 15 recounts the crucial moment when the apostles and elders determined that Gentile believers were not required to undergo circumcision or take on full Torah observance. The apostles ruled that Gentiles should abstain from four specific practices: idolatry, blood, meat of strangled animals, and sexual immorality (Acts 15:20, Leviticus 17-18).

These restrictions align with the basic ethical standards of Leviticus 17–18, which were historically applied to sojourners in Israel. The implication was clear: Gentiles do not need to become Jews to be part of the *ekklesia*. This decision preserved both the unity of the body and the particular identity of Jewish believers.

Some argue that this council was merely a temporary solution or a minimal entry point. But Paul, who was present at the council, repeatedly taught that Gentiles are justified by faith, not by works of the Torah (Galatians 2:16). Yet, he never taught Jews to abandon Torah. In fact, he himself continued to live as an observant Jew (Acts 21:24).

One Law? Or One Covenant with Distinct Callings?

The Torah does include the statement that there is "one law for you and for the stranger," but it also includes numerous commandments that apply only to specific groups—priests, men, women, lepers, Nazirites, and yes, native-born Israelites. Leviticus and Numbers make these distinctions clear.

In other words, "one law" is not "identical practice." The Torah itself assumes diversity within unity. Jewish calling involves a deeper and broader obligation to *mitzvot*—not because Jews are superior, but because they are covenantally marked by Sinai.

Gentile believers are not inferior for not taking on the yoke of Torah. They are co-heirs, fellow citizens, and full participants in the life of the Messiah. The unity of the Body is not achieved by uniformity but by mutual respect and interdependence (1 Corinthians 12:12–27).

Problems with the "One Law Movement"

The modern One Law Movement, sometimes associated with Hebrew Roots ideology, often advocates for full Torah observance for all believers, including circumcision, dietary laws, and festival observance as mandatory. While often well-intentioned, this movement risks undermining both the New Testament witness and Jewish covenantal identity.

It collapses the distinction between Jew and Gentile that the New Testament seeks to preserve. It often ignores or minimizes Jewish historical suffering and theological vocation. And it distorts the nature of Gentile inclusion, making Torah observance a prerequisite for full belonging.

Moreover, this movement often exhibits anti-traditional bias, rejecting Rabbinic Judaism wholesale and elevating their own interpretations of Torah. In doing so, they inadvertently create a new form of legalism—binding Gentiles to laws not given to them.

A Bilateral Path Forward

Messianic Judaism affirms the legitimacy of Torah-observant Jewish life in Yeshua and also the freedom of Gentile believers to follow the Spirit without taking on full Jewish obligations. This bilateral ecclesiology is not a compromise—it is a return to the apostolic pattern.

The Gentile believer can honor Jewish time, study Torah, and draw from Jewish practice without claiming Jewish identity. The Jewish believer can remain faithful to ancestral covenant obligations without demanding uniformity.

This model also allows for respectful cooperation with the broader Jewish world. It affirms that Torah is not a burden but a gift—a sacred trust given to Israel. As Paul says, "To them belong the adoption and the glory and the covenants and the giving of the *Torah* and the Temple service and the promises" (Romans 9:4).

Conclusion: Distinction in Unity

The Torah is not a flat code but a dynamic covenant. It establishes principles of holiness, justice, and mercy while distinguishing roles and responsibilities. Messianic faith upholds both the unity of the Body and the diversity of its members.

To insist on "one law" in a rigid, identical sense is to flatten God's beautiful design.

Instead, we are invited into a shared life where Jew and Gentile, male and female, slave and free are one in Messiah—each bringing their own story, tradition, and obedience to the table (Galatians 3:28).

One Messiah. One Spirit. One faith. But a diversity of callings, bound together in love.

Reflection and Discussion Questions:

- What does the phrase "one law for all" mean in its biblical context?

- Why is it important to preserve Jewish distinctiveness within the Body of Messiah?

- What are the theological and relational problems with the One Law Movement?

- How does Acts 15 model a bilateral approach to unity and diversity?

- In what ways can Gentile believers engage with Torah without assuming Jewish identity?

Chapter 7:
Jewish Life Cycle in Messianic Perspective

The Jewish life cycle is not merely a collection of rituals but a sacred rhythm woven into the fabric of Jewish identity. From birth to death, these ceremonies mark spiritual transitions and covenantal milestones. For Messianic Jews, these traditional rites are infused with new depth through faith in Yeshua, the Messiah. Rather than discarding the customs of our forefathers, we seek to understand and fulfill them in light of the New Covenant. This chapter will explore the key stages of the Jewish life cycle—birth, circumcision, coming of age, marriage, and death—within a Messianic framework, examining how these ancient traditions continue to speak powerfully today.

Birth and Covenant: Welcoming a New Soul

In Jewish tradition, the birth of a child is a moment of great joy and divine encounter. The Talmud teaches that a newborn brings with them a portion of divine breath, a spark of heaven entering into the world.[1] This echoes the Genesis account in which God breathes life into Adam (Genesis 2:7). In Messianic understanding, this birth is not only physical but also a sign of ongoing covenantal faithfulness: "For the promise is for you and your children" (Acts 2:39).

---

[1] Babylonian Talmud, Niddah 30b.

Brit Milah and Naming

For boys, the *brit milah* (covenant of circumcision) is performed on the eighth day in obedience to Genesis 17:12. This commandment, given to Abraham, marks the entry of a Jewish male into the Abrahamic covenant. In Messianic Judaism, *brit milah* is honored as a sign of continuity with Israel's identity. Paul, though he opposed circumcision for Gentiles, affirmed its value for Jews (Romans 3:1–2).

For girls, the naming ceremony (*simchat bat*) is a more recent development in Jewish tradition, often held at home or in the synagogue. The naming affirms the child's connection to her people and to the biblical matriarchs. Messianic communities frequently incorporate blessings from Luke 2, where Yeshua is presented at the Temple, affirming the holiness of newborn life and covenant presentation (Luke 2:21–24).

Coming of Age: Bar and Bat Mitzvah

At age 13 for boys and 12 for girls, Jewish children become *bar* or *bat mitzvah*—"sons" or "daughters" of the commandment. This is not a graduation from Judaism but a formal acceptance of personal responsibility for Torah observance. Traditionally, the young person reads from the Torah and the Haftarah, affirming their place in the covenant community.

In Messianic congregations, *bar* and *bat mitzvah* ceremonies retain their traditional structure while incorporating the *Brit Chadashah* (New Testament). A young person may also read from a gospel portion or reflect on Yeshua's role as the living Torah. Just as Yeshua was found in the Temple at age 12, asking questions and demonstrating understanding (Luke 2:46–49), so too Messianic youth are encouraged to deepen their faith and knowledge.

Mark Kinzer notes that this stage marks the development of covenantal consciousness.[2] It is not merely a religious rite, but a moment of identity affirmation— "I am a Jew, and I follow the God of Israel through His Messiah." It is also a declaration of intergenerational continuity, linking a young person with both their people and their spiritual inheritance.

Marriage: A Covenant of Joy and Responsibility

Marriage in Judaism is called *kiddushin*, or sanctification. It is more than a contract; it is a holy covenant modeled on God's relationship with Israel. The wedding ceremony is filled with symbolism: the *chuppah* (canopy) represents the home being built; the *ketubah* (marriage contract) formalizes responsibilities; and the breaking of the glass symbolizes both joy and the ongoing exile.

Messianic weddings follow the traditional Jewish structure while honoring Yeshua as the center of the union. The presence of Messiah is invoked through prayer, Scripture, and the sanctification of the marriage as a picture of the bride and bridegroom in Revelation 19:7–9.

Paul calls marriage a "great mystery," referring to Messiah and the *ekklesia* (Ephesians 5:32). This metaphor draws directly from Jewish imagery of God as the husband of Israel (Hosea 2:19–20). Thus, Messianic weddings are covenantal, communal, and prophetic. They proclaim not only love between two people, but God's enduring love for His people.

---

[2] Mark Kinzer, *Postmissionary Messianic Judaism* (Grand Rapids: Brazos Press, 2005).

Aging, Death, and Hope in the Resurrection

Jewish tradition sees aging as a crown of honor: "Gray hair is a crown of glory; it is gained by living a righteous life" (Proverbs 16:31). Elders are respected for their wisdom and remembered in community. As life wanes, Jewish custom encourages *teshuvah* (repentance), the giving of *tzedakah* (charity), and the recitation of the Shema.

Upon death, the body is treated with reverence. The *chevra kadisha* (holy society) prepares the body for burial. In Messianic settings, this is accompanied by Scripture readings, prayers in Yeshua's name, and the proclamation of resurrection hope. As Paul declares, "The dead in Messiah shall rise first" (1 Thessalonians 4:16).

The *Kaddish*—the mourner's prayer—never mentions death. Instead, it praises God and longs for His kingdom. This reflects a Messianic perspective: that even in death, the final word belongs to God. The return of Messiah will bring about the resurrection of the dead and the reunification of the faithful.

The Cycle Continues: Redemption in Every Season

What emerges from the Jewish life cycle is a pattern of sanctification. Every stage of life is an opportunity for covenantal affirmation. Messianic Judaism does not reject these customs but redeems them in Messiah.

Faith in Yeshua does not remove Jewish identity—it completes it. Just as circumcision, *bar mitzvah*, marriage, and burial point to deeper spiritual realities, so too do they proclaim that the God of Israel is faithful from generation to generation. Each stage becomes a shadow of the greater redemptive story unfolding through Israel's Messiah.

Reflection and Discussion Questions:

- How do the life cycle events reinforce Jewish identity and covenantal continuity?

- What does it mean to celebrate traditional rites through the lens of the New Covenant?

- In what ways can Messianic communities honor Jewish tradition without compromising faith in Yeshua?

- How do marriage and burial reflect both Jewish and Messianic theology?

- What can the Jewish life cycle teach the broader Body of Messiah about sanctifying time and life?

Chapter 8:
Individual vs. Communal – A Messianic Tension

One of the most profound tensions in the spiritual life is the balance between the individual and the community. In Western culture, shaped by Enlightenment ideals, the individual often reigns supreme. Personal autonomy, private faith, and self- determination are seen as core values. In contrast, Jewish tradition—and by extension, Messianic Jewish theology—emphasizes the communal. From the Sinai covenant to the synagogue, from mourning to celebration, Judaism is rooted in peoplehood. This chapter explores the dynamic between individual and communal identity through a Messianic lens, asking what it means to be both personally redeemed and corporately called.

The Individual Before God

The Bible contains many examples of personal relationship with God: Abraham walks with God, Moses speaks with Him face-to-face, David cries out in the Psalms. These figures demonstrate that each person must encounter God individually. Salvation, in a sense, is personal. Each soul is accountable before God (Ezekiel 18:20). Yeshua Himself calls individuals to discipleship: "Come, follow Me" (Matthew 4:19).

Paul reinforces this when he says, "Each of us will give an account of himself to God" (Romans 14:12). Faith in Yeshua begins with an individual decision, a response to the personal call of Messiah. This aligns with the prophetic call for inner circumcision of the heart (Deuteronomy 10:16; Jeremiah 31:33).

Yet, this personal calling never exists in a vacuum. In Scripture, individuals are called *into* a people, not *away* from one. Abraham is called to become a great nation. Israel is redeemed as a collective. The covenant at Sinai is made not with isolated persons but with a gathered people (Exodus 19:5–6).

The Weight of the Community in Judaism

Rabbinic Judaism has long affirmed that "all Israel is responsible for one another" (Talmud, *Shevuot* 39a).[1] Communal identity is inseparable from Jewish life. A *minyan* (quorum of ten) is required for many prayers, including the Kaddish. Mourning is not endured alone; it is shared in *shiva*. Feasts are not private dinners but national celebrations.

Even repentance is communal. On *Yom Kippur*, Jews confess not only personal sins but those of the nation: "We have sinned, we have transgressed." This confession, using the first-person plural, reinforces the corporate aspect of *teshuvah*. The community stands together before God.

Messianic Judaism, rooted in this tradition, affirms that salvation is not merely the rescue of isolated souls, but the redemption of a people. Yeshua died not just for "me," but for Israel and the nations. As the angel told Joseph, "He will save His people from their sins" (Matthew 1:21).

---

[1] Babylonian Talmud, Shevuot 39a.

Ecclesiology and the People of God

The New Testament uses collective language to describe believers: "you are a royal priesthood, a holy nation" (1 Peter 2:9). Paul calls the community the "Body of Messiah," with many members working together (1 Corinthians 12). No member can say to the other, "I have no need of you."

In this Body, Jews and Gentiles are one, yet not the same. Kinzer's bilateral ecclesiology teaches that unity does not require uniformity.[2] Jews retain their covenantal identity, while Gentiles are grafted in as fellow heirs. The Body is diverse, covenantally distinct, yet spiritually united.

This theological framework resists both hyper-individualism and forced assimilation. It affirms that faith is personal but never private. One belongs to the Messiah and also to His people. Thus, spiritual maturity is measured not only by personal devotion, but by covenantal participation in community life.

The Dangers of Over-Individualism

In modern religious culture, the community is often seen as optional. Faith is reduced to personal experience, often detached from tradition, accountability, or shared responsibility. Yet this mindset is foreign to both Scripture and Jewish thought.

Without community, discipleship falters. Yeshua trained His disciples in community.

Paul planted congregations, not just converts. The early Messianic believers were "together, having everything in

---

[2] Mark Kinzer, *Postmissionary Messianic Judaism.*

common" (Acts 2:44). They broke bread in homes, prayed together in the Temple, and shared resources.

Over-individualism leads to theological distortion. It fosters consumeristic faith, where believers attend services as spectators rather than participants. It erodes identity, especially for Jewish believers, whose faith must remain tied to peoplehood.

The Power of Community in Messianic Life

Community is not merely a support system; it is the embodiment of covenant. It is in community that the Torah is read, prayers are said, and justice is pursued. It is where we celebrate births, mourn deaths, and sanctify time.

Messianic communities stand as a testimony that Yeshua has not nullified Jewish communal life but fulfilled its spiritual intent. The *Shabbat* table, with candles, *challah*, and blessing, becomes a place of sacred memory and prophetic hope. Festivals like Passover or *Sukkot* become not only historical commemorations but anticipations of the Messianic Kingdom.

Gentile believers in these communities are not guests— they are fellow citizens. Yet the community honors Jewish space, affirms Jewish distinction, and protects Jewish continuity. As Paul says, the Gentiles are fellow heirs, not co-opted Israelites (Ephesians 2:19–22).

Conclusion: A Covenant People, Not Just Private Believers

Messianic life calls for a radical reorientation from "me" to "we." We are saved individually, but we live covenantally. Our faith is not abstract—it is embodied in the community of the redeemed.

The tension between individual and communal identity will always remain. Yet in that tension lies the beauty of God's design: persons uniquely called, gathered into a people chosen to bear His name.

<u>Reflection and Discussion Questions:</u>

- Why is it important to maintain a balance between personal faith and communal responsibility?

- In what ways has modern culture distorted biblical models of community?

- How does bilateral ecclesiology help preserve both Jewish identity and unity in Messiah?

- What are practical ways to strengthen Messianic community life today?

- How does the Torah shape not only individual obedience but collective sanctity?

Chapter 9:
Hebrew vs. Greek Thinking – Two Worldviews in Conflict and Harmony

At the heart of many theological misunderstandings and cultural tensions within the Body of Messiah lies a fundamental clash of worldviews: the Hebraic mindset versus the Hellenistic (Greek) mindset. These two paradigms—one rooted in the biblical world of Israel and the other in classical philosophy—have profoundly shaped Western civilization, including Christianity. In Messianic Judaism, recovering a Hebraic worldview is not just a return to roots; it is a necessary correction to centuries of spiritual misalignment. This chapter explores the defining features of each worldview, how they influenced the Church, and how a Messianic perspective brings reconciliation and clarity.

Origins of the Conflict

The Hebrew worldview is relational, holistic, and grounded in covenant. It emphasizes obedience, community, and action. Truth is not merely something to be known but something to be lived. In contrast, the Greek worldview— shaped by philosophers like Plato and Aristotle—is analytical, abstract, and dualistic. It elevates reason over revelation and the spiritual over the material.

In the biblical narrative, Hebrew thought unfolds through story, symbol, and lived experience. God reveals Himself not as an abstract force but as "I Am"—personal, present, and faithful. Greek thought seeks timeless truths detached from context. The body is often seen as inferior to the soul, and salvation is framed as escape from materiality rather than the redemption of it.

This contrast is seen as early as the Hellenization of Judea under Alexander the Great. The Maccabean revolt was not only a political struggle but a resistance against the imposition of Greek thought and values. The Jewish people fought not merely to preserve their temple but their worldview.

Language as Worldview

Language reflects worldview. Hebrew is a verb-based, action-oriented language. Words are concrete, earthy, and relational. For example, the Hebrew word for "know" (*yada*) implies intimacy and personal experience (Genesis 4:1). In contrast, Greek often treats knowledge as intellectual comprehension (*gnosis*).

This is why Scripture written in Hebrew has a different texture than its Greek translation, the Septuagint (LXX). When Hebrew thought is translated into Greek, some of its nuances are lost or reshaped. This is evident in theological vocabulary—terms like *logos* (word), *sarx* (flesh), and *pneuma* (spirit) carry Hellenistic baggage when read outside their Jewish context.

Greek Influence on the Early Church

By the second and third centuries CE, the Church was increasingly dominated by Gentile believers raised in Greek culture. Early Church Fathers like Justin Martyr, Origen, and Augustine interpreted Scripture through Greek philosophical lenses. Augustine's embrace of Neoplatonism, for instance, led to a dualistic view of body and soul, grace and law, spirit and matter.

This philosophical shift introduced key theological distortions:

- The Torah was reinterpreted as legalistic rather than covenantal.

- Israel was spiritualized or replaced by the Church.

- The resurrection became less about bodily restoration and more about disembodied bliss.

- Yeshua was discussed in metaphysical categories rather than in covenantal terms.

In this context, Messianic Jews became increasingly marginalized. Their Torah- observance was seen as backward. The Hebraic roots of the faith were cut off in favor of Greek rationalism.

The Hebraic Mind of Yeshua

Yeshua was not a Greek philosopher. He was a Jewish rabbi speaking in parables, rooted in Torah, and expressing truth through action. His teaching style was narrative, midrashic, and participatory. He taught not abstract principles but concrete applications of God's will.

When He said, "Blessed are the peacemakers," He did not mean inner tranquility (as in Stoic philosophy), but active reconciliation rooted in God's *shalom*. When He called for "belief," it was not assent to propositions but covenantal faithfulness.

Even the term *Messiah*—so central to the New

Testament—is a Hebraic concept, not a Greek one. It speaks of anointed kingship, deliverance, and restoration of Israel. To understand Yeshua rightly is to interpret Him through Jewish categories.

Paul: A Case Study in Integration

Paul is often misunderstood as a Hellenistic theologian. Yet, he was a Pharisee, trained under Rabbi Gamaliel (Acts 22:3). His letters, though written in Greek, are saturated with Hebraic structure, idiom, and logic. Paul argues like a rabbi, not a Greek logician.

When Paul contrasts "law" and "grace," he is not rejecting Torah but opposing legalism and ethnocentrism as paths to righteousness. He insists on faith working through love (Galatians 5:6), a profoundly Hebraic ethic.

As Messianic Jewish scholar David Stern explains, Paul's writing must be interpreted "not against the background of Greek philosophy but against the background of Jewish thought and halakhic reasoning." [1]

Messianic Judaism: Restoring the Balance

Messianic Judaism offers a prophetic correction to centuries of Greek distortion. It restores the Hebrew worldview of Scripture, reconnects theology to covenant, and insists that faith be lived in time, body, and community.

In this framework:

- Salvation is not escape from the world but its

---

[1] David Stern, *Restoring the Jewishness of the Gospel* (Jewish New Testament Publications, 1992).

redemption (Romans 8:21).

- Torah is not legalism but instruction in holy living (Psalm 19:7).

- Worship is not only private but communal, embodied, and liturgical.

- Discipleship is not mastering doctrine but following the Master in obedience.

The feasts, Sabbaths, dietary laws, and lifecycle events all become touchpoints where theology is lived. In remembering Passover, we recall God's redemptive acts. In keeping *Shabbat*, we affirm creation and covenant. In circumcision, we mark belonging. All of this resists the abstracting tendency of Greek thinking.

Relevance for Today

In a postmodern age, where secularism and hyper-individualism reign, the Hebrew mindset offers a grounding alternative. It calls believers back to community, tradition, and concrete action. It challenges theologies that separate body and spirit, belief and obedience, faith and culture.

For Gentile believers, embracing a Hebraic worldview does not mean becoming Jews, but recovering the roots of their faith. It means seeing Scripture not as a system of doctrines, but a story of covenantal love. It means honoring Israel's unique calling while living in solidarity with her Messiah.

For Jewish believers, it affirms that one can follow Yeshua without abandoning the rich heritage of Judaism. It is a way of continuity, not replacement.

Conclusion: A Whole Gospel Requires a Whole Worldview

The gospel of the kingdom is not a philosophical idea—it is a lived reality. It involves time, body, ritual, memory, and community. To recover the fullness of the good news, the Church must return to its Hebraic roots.

Greek and Hebrew thought need not be enemies. There is beauty in logic, art, and structure. But theology must begin and end in the world of Israel's Scriptures. Only then will we understand the heart of God, the mission of Messiah, and the call of His people.

Reflection and Discussion Questions:

- What are the main differences between Greek and Hebrew ways of thinking?

- How has Greek philosophy influenced traditional Christian theology?

- In what ways did Yeshua's teachings reflect a Hebraic worldview?

- How does Messianic Judaism restore balance between theology and lived experience?

- How can Gentile believers embrace a Hebraic worldview without appropriating Jewish identity?

Chapter 10:
Greek Brain, Hebrew Brain – A Tale of Two Ways of Knowing

In our journey to rediscover the Jewish roots of faith, one of the most overlooked yet transformative insights is the recognition of how the brain itself is shaped by culture and worldview. The phrase "Greek brain, Hebrew brain" is not about ethnicity or genetics— it's about how we perceive, learn, reason, and relate. Greek and Hebrew cultures shaped very different approaches to knowledge and truth. Understanding these cognitive frameworks helps us appreciate why the early Church evolved as it did, and how recovering a Hebraic mindset can bring greater unity between heart, mind, and spirit.

Left Brain vs. Right Brain: A Metaphor for Worldview

Neurologists have long discussed the differing functions of the brain's hemispheres. While overly simplified, the left brain is often associated with logic, language, and analytical thinking, whereas the right brain is linked to imagination, emotion, and holistic perception. Greek culture heavily favored left-brain traits: rationality, categorization, and intellectual abstraction. Hebrew thought, in contrast, was deeply right-brained: poetic, narrative, embodied, and intuitive.

This difference mirrors the cultural ways in which the Greeks and Hebrews approached life and theology. Greeks sought to define God in terms of essence, attributes, and logic. Hebrews encountered God in stories, actions, and lived obedience. Greek theology is systematic; Hebrew theology is relational. Greek religion abstracts; Hebrew faith incarnates.

Greek Brain: Philosophy, Abstraction, and Dualism

The Greek mind seeks clarity through categorization. From Plato to Aristotle, Greek philosophy aimed to reduce the world to understandable systems. Truth was discovered through reason, debated in academies, and recorded in treatises. This influenced early Christian theology profoundly, especially through thinkers like Clement, Origen, and Augustine.

This Greek "brain" often divides reality into binaries: body/soul, sacred/secular, heaven/earth. The material world is seen as imperfect, and salvation as escape from it. This led to an emphasis on afterlife over present obedience, on belief over behavior, and on dogma over discipleship.

Greek Christianity became creedal and hierarchical. The Church became an institution of theological correctness rather than a community of covenant faithfulness. Worship became cerebral and liturgical, removed from daily life. Salvation was viewed primarily as a legal transaction, not a relational transformation.

Hebrew Brain: Story, Symbol, and Covenant

In contrast, the Hebrew brain embraces ambiguity, story, and process. Truth is not defined but revealed. Torah is not a textbook of laws but a narrative of love, covenant, failure, and redemption. Hebrew thought values memory over logic, obedience over speculation, and community over individuality.

This is why Scripture tells stories instead of presenting systematic theology. Abraham's life teaches covenant.

David's psalms model worship. The Exodus is the prototype of redemption. The Hebrew brain asks not "What is true in theory?" but "What does God require of me today?"

Rabbinic thought reflects this complexity. Talmudic discussions often leave questions unresolved. Debate is seen not as a weakness but a sign of maturity. The sages prized *halakhah*—walking out the Torah—more than abstract theology.

The Mind of Messiah

Yeshua embodied the Hebrew brain. He taught in parables, used imagery from everyday life, and called for action more than intellectual assent. He never wrote a doctrinal treatise but formed disciples who lived with Him in community.

His greatest commandment was not a creed but a call: "Love *ADONAI* your God with all your heart and with all your soul and with all your strength" (Deuteronomy 6:5). He engaged hearts before minds. His miracles were not philosophical proofs but embodied signs of the kingdom.

When Paul urged believers to have the "mind of Messiah" (1 Corinthians 2:16), he wasn't asking them to become Greek philosophers but Hebraic disciples—people who think covenantally, live obediently, and love relationally.

The Effects on Discipleship and Theology

The dominance of the Greek brain in Christian history has led to several distortions:

- Discipleship became knowledge-based rather than obedience-based.

- Salvation was discussed as a legal contract instead of a transformative relationship.

- Faith was treated as private belief instead of public covenant.

In many churches today, theology is taught like philosophy: abstract, systematic, disconnected from community. But in Jewish and Messianic practice, theology is baked into the rhythm of life. *Shabbat* is theology. Passover is theology. Mourning and celebration, food and fasting—all express what we believe.

Messianic Judaism: A Whole-Brain Faith

Messianic Judaism calls us to reintegrate the fragmented brain. We are not to abandon reason, but neither are we to idolize it. True discipleship engages both sides of the brain: the analytical and the artistic, the logical and the lyrical.

In a Messianic context:

- Torah study involves head and heart.

- Community life models covenant.

- Worship is both liturgical and spontaneous.

- Revelation is welcomed not just in doctrine, but in encounter.

Children learn not just facts but rituals. Elders are valued for stories, not degrees. A "whole-brain" faith sees God in the text and in the table, in study and in song.

Restoring a Hebraic Cognitive Framework

In our modern, digital age, the Greek brain is further reinforced by screen culture, abstraction, and disembodied information. The Church—and especially Messianic communities—must intentionally re-form people through embodied, covenantal, communal practices.

This means:

- Emphasizing story over principle.

- Valuing experience alongside knowledge.

- Teaching theology through practice: keeping feasts, celebrating life-cycle events, living out generosity and justice.

In Jewish tradition, to "know" something is to be changed by it. In Messianic life, to "believe" something is to walk in it. A Hebrew brain doesn't just hear the word—it does the word (James 1:22).

Conclusion: Becoming Disciples of the Whole Gospel

To follow Yeshua faithfully, we must recover His way of thinking. We need a "renewed mind" (Romans 12:2), not shaped by the world—or by Greek categories—but by the Spirit and the Scriptures.

This chapter invites us to live a holistic, whole-brain discipleship. Let us be people who love God with heart and mind, who think biblically, walk communally, and worship incarnationally. Let the Hebrew brain guide our theology, our practice, and our identity in Messiah.

<u>Reflection and Discussion Questions:</u>

- What are key features of the Greek and Hebrew ways of thinking?

- How has the "Greek brain" influenced the Western Church?

- In what ways does Messianic Judaism restore the "Hebrew brain" approach to faith?

- How can we intentionally disciple others using both head and heart?

- What changes can you make in your study, worship, or community life to embrace a Hebraic mindset more fully?

Chapter 11: Difficult Passages – Wrestling with the Word in a Messianic Key

One of the most enduring hallmarks of both Judaism and Messianic faith is the willingness to wrestle with Scripture. From Jacob's night-long struggle with the angel to the sages of the Talmud probing every jot and tittle of the Torah, Jewish tradition has always embraced difficulty as the birthplace of revelation. Messianic Judaism continues this tradition by refusing to flatten Scripture's tensions or erase its ambiguities. Instead, we enter into them, bringing with us the insights of the Tanakh, the teachings of Yeshua, and the deep wells of both Jewish and Christian interpretation.

In this chapter, we explore some of the most "difficult passages" in the Bible—those texts that seem to contradict other verses, challenge theological assumptions, or present ethical dilemmas. We approach them with humility, reverence, and faith in the goodness and wisdom of God's Word. Drawing on your sermon notes and supplemented by historical and scholarly resources, this chapter provides Messianic insights into why these difficult texts matter and how we can read them redemptively.

Reading as Struggle: The Jewish Context

Within Jewish tradition, challenging texts are not seen as problems to be solved but as invitations to deeper engagement. The Talmud says, "Turn it, and turn it, for everything is in it" (Pirkei Avot 5:22). Wrestling with the

Word is a sacred task. Rabbinic literature is filled with debates about seemingly contradictory laws, narratives, or theological principles—yet rarely does it seek to eliminate those tensions. Instead, multiple perspectives are often preserved in the same text.

For example, the sages preserved the dispute between Hillel and Shammai throughout much of the Mishnah and Talmud. This plurality is seen as honoring the multifaceted wisdom of God. As Messianic believers, we inherit not only the Bible but also this interpretive tradition of respectful engagement with complexity.

The Problem of Divine Violence

Perhaps no issue is more troubling for modern readers than divine violence in the Hebrew Scriptures. Passages such as the command to destroy the Canaanites (Deuteronomy 20:16–18) or the death of Uzzah for touching the Ark (2 Samuel 6:6–7) provoke deep discomfort. How can a God of mercy order—or permit—such acts?

One approach is to place these events within the historical and covenantal context. The Canaanite nations practiced extreme idolatry, including child sacrifice (Deuteronomy 12:31). Israel was commanded not to conquer for imperial gain but to cleanse the land from evil. Furthermore, divine justice in Scripture is not arbitrary—it is consistent with God's holiness and Israel's mission as a priestly nation (Exodus 19:6).

Messianic scholars like Michael Brown argue that the conquest narratives must be read through the lens of God's long-suffering mercy and the progressive revelation of His plan of redemption.[1] Yeshua's teachings in the New Covenant do not erase divine judgment but place it within the broader arc of repentance and renewal.

Paul and the Law: Apparent Contradictions

Paul is often cited as teaching that "the law is abolished" (Ephesians 2:15), which seems to contradict Torah observance and Yeshua's own words in Matthew 5:17: "Do not think that I came to abolish the Torah." How do we reconcile these?

A careful Messianic reading sees Paul not as rejecting Torah but defining its function in the life of gentile disciples of Messiah. Ephesians 2:15 refers to "the law code of *mitzvot* contained in regulations," likely referring to man-made *halakhot* (legal rulings) that created ethnic division between Jew and Gentile. Paul's larger point is that Yeshua has created one new humanity, not by canceling Torah, but by removing the legalistic, traditional, man-made barrier that excluded Gentiles from fellowship.

Romans 3:31 affirms: "Do we then nullify the Torah through faithfulness? May it never be! On the contrary, we uphold the Torah." Paul's critique is against legalism and misuse of the Torah as a means of earning salvation, not Torah itself.[2]

David Stern observes that Paul "uses the word 'law' in multiple ways, and most errors arise from failing to ask which sense is intended in a given passage."[3] In this light,

---

[1] Michael L. Brown, *Answering Jewish Objections to Jesus, Vol. 1* (Baker Books, 2000), 94–100.
[2] Romans 3:31; Galatians 2:21.
[3] David H. Stern, *Jewish New Testament Commentary* (Jewish New

Messianic interpretation carefully distinguishes between Torah as covenantal instruction and Torah as misapplied legalism.

Women in Leadership

Another challenging area is the role of women in Scripture. Passages like 1 Timothy 2:12 ("But I do not allow a woman to train or dictate to a man, but to be in a quiet demeanor") seem to restrict women's leadership. Yet Scripture also presents prophetesses like Deborah, Huldah, and Anna, and apostles such as Junia (Romans 16:7).

Messianic Judaism tends to affirm women's leadership as rooted in biblical precedent and consistent with Yeshua's practice. He taught women (Luke 10:39), defended them (John 8:11), and commissioned them as witnesses to His resurrection (Matthew 28:10). The cultural background of Paul's letters reveals that many of his prohibitions were context-specific—addressing issues of order and false teaching in particular congregations.

As in Judaism, Messianic communities often understand authority as communal and covenantal rather than hierarchical. Leadership is rooted in gifting and service, not gender alone.

The Fate of the Unevangelized

What about those who have never heard the gospel? Does their ignorance doom them?

This question has troubled theologians for centuries. Paul's teaching in Romans 1:18–20 states that God's

---

Testament Publications, 1996), 340.

invisible qualities are evident in creation, making humanity "without excuse." Yet in Romans 2:14–16, Paul suggests that Gentiles who follow their conscience may be judged righteously.

Messianic Jewish theology affirms that God is just and merciful. Salvation is always through Yeshua (Acts 4:12), but judgment considers revelation received. As Abraham said, "Will not the Judge of all the earth do right?" (Genesis 18:25).

The Tanakh hints at a wider mercy. Melchizedek, Jethro, and Job were non-Israelites who knew God. The prophetic vision includes Gentile nations turning to Adonai (Isaiah 2:2–4). Our task is not to resolve every mystery but to trust in God's character and proclaim the good news to all.

Predestination and Free Will

Another tension arises between divine sovereignty and human responsibility. Verses like Romans 9:18 ("He hardens whom He wills") seem to suggest predestination, while others command repentance and faith (Acts 17:30).

Jewish tradition affirms both divine foreknowledge and human choice. The Mishnah says, "Everything is foreseen, yet freedom is granted" (*Pirkei Avot* 3:15). Messianic interpretation sees this not as a contradiction but a mystery— God is sovereign, yet He dignifies human agency. Yeshua weeps over Jerusalem, lamenting their refusal to respond (Luke 13:34), underscoring that divine compassion desires human partnership.

The Hard Sayings of Yeshua

Yeshua Himself uttered many difficult statements: "hate

his own father, mother, wife, children, brothers, and sisters" (Luke 14:26), "be perfect, just as your Father in heaven is perfect" (Matthew 5:48), and "Sell all, as much as you have" (Luke 18:22). These sayings are often misunderstood when removed from their Jewish rhetorical context.

In Semitic hyperbole, "hate" means to prefer less. Yeshua calls for allegiance to God above family—not emotional hatred.[4] Perfection refers to maturity and wholeness, not flawlessness. The call to sell possessions addresses one man's idolatry of wealth, not a universal command.

Messianic interpretation seeks to hear Yeshua as His Jewish audience would: in layers, with metaphor, urgency, and covenantal depth.

Why Difficult Passages Matter

Rather than threatening faith, difficult passages deepen it. They remind us that Scripture is not a manual but a living Word. It resists simplification, demands engagement, and shapes character through struggle.

As Messianic believers, we are called to model a robust, reverent wrestling with the Word—neither dismissing the hard parts nor reducing them to slogans. The tradition of *drash* (searching) teaches us to mine every verse for hidden treasure. As the Psalmist says, "The unfolding of Your words gives light" (Psalm 119:130).

---

[4] Cf. Genesis 29:30–31, where "hated" (Heb. *sane*) means "loved less."

Conclusion: Wrestling Toward Wisdom

Difficult passages are not obstacles to faith; they are invitations to go deeper. Like Jacob, we wrestle through the night and emerge with a limp—and a blessing. The Word shapes us not just in what we understand but in what we seek.

In a Messianic key, we embrace complexity not as a threat but as a sign of Scripture's divine origin. We are not called to master the Word but to be mastered by it. In the questions, we find connection. In the struggle, we find the face of God.

Reflection and Discussion Questions:

- What passage of Scripture have you found personally difficult? How has your understanding of it changed?

- How does Jewish tradition help us engage more faithfully with textual tension?

- How can we avoid oversimplifying difficult verses in the New Testament?

- Why is it important for Messianic believers to wrestle with these passages communally, not just individually?

- What does it mean to be "mastered by the Word" rather than trying to master it?

Chapter 12:
The Development of Anti-Jewish Theology – A Tragic Departure from the Olive Tree

The relationship between the Church and the Jewish people is a story of profound theological beauty and equally profound historical sorrow. From a shared beginning in Jerusalem, where Yeshua's first followers were devout Jews, the ecclesia eventually drifted not only from its Hebraic roots but also from the Jewish people themselves. Over centuries, this drift turned into rejection, and rejection hardened into doctrine. This chapter explores the development of anti-Jewish theology—often called supersessionism or replacement theology—its causes, consequences, and how Messianic Judaism confronts and seeks to heal these wounds.

Beginnings: Unity in the First Century

The first generation of believers in Yeshua were exclusively Jewish. Acts 2 describes thousands of Jews in Jerusalem coming to faith during *Shavu'ot* (Pentecost). These early followers did not see themselves as leaving Judaism but as living its fulfillment. The apostles continued to worship in the Temple, participate in synagogue life, and teach Torah observance in light of Yeshua's messiahship (Acts 3:1; 21:20).

Gentiles were grafted into this community through faith in Messiah and the work of the Spirit (Acts 10; Romans 11).

The apostolic community struggled—creatively and prayerfully—to maintain unity amid diversity, as seen in Acts 15 and Paul's epistles.

Paul described this new body as "one new man" (Ephesians 2:15), not through erasing distinctions, but through reconciliation.

The Separation Begins: Political and Social Pressures

The destruction of the Second Temple in 70 CE and the *Bar Kokhba* revolt in 135 CE were turning points. After the Roman devastation of Judea, Jews became politically and socially marginalized across the empire. At the same time, the growing Gentile Church was eager to distance itself from a persecuted minority.

Under these pressures, Christian leaders began to redefine their faith in ways that distanced it from Judaism. Justin Martyr (c. 100–165 CE) was one of the first to articulate replacement theology. In his *Dialogue with Trypho*, he argued that the Church was the "true Israel" and that the Mosaic covenant was obsolete.

The Rise of Supersessionism

By the fourth century, this perspective had hardened into dogma. Church Fathers such as Tertullian, Origen, and especially Augustine further developed the idea that the Church had replaced Israel. Augustine wrote that the Jews were a "witness people"— preserved in dispersion as proof of God's judgment. This doctrine served to delegitimize Jewish religious practice while justifying Christian triumphalism.

The Council of Nicaea in 325 CE, convened by

Constantine, marked a decisive break. Not only did it define key doctrines apart from Jewish input, but it also established a Christian calendar separate from the Jewish festivals. In a letter, Constantine wrote:

"Let us then have nothing in common with the detestable Jewish crowd."[1]

Anti-Jewish rhetoric became embedded in liturgy, homilies, and canon law. Laws were enacted prohibiting Jewish-Christian marriages, banning Jews from holding office, and forbidding converts from observing Torah.[2]

Consequences: Theology Turned Tragedy

The consequences of anti-Jewish theology were devastating. It fueled centuries of persecution—pogroms, expulsions, forced conversions, and eventually, the theological groundwork for the Holocaust. When Christian Europe turned violently against the Jewish people, it often did so with theological justification.

Martin Luther, initially sympathetic to Jews, later wrote *On the Jews and Their Lies*, in which he called for the burning of synagogues and Jewish homes. His writings were later used by the Nazis to legitimize their genocidal policies.[3]

This tragic history demands more than regret—it calls for repentance and theological correction.

---

[1] Constantine, Letter to the Churches, Eusebius, *Life of Constantine* 3.18.
[2] Jeremy Cohen, *Living Letters of the Law* (University of California Press, 1999), 64–70.
[3] Martin Luther, On the Jews and Their Lies (1543).

Theological Fault Lines

Several theological missteps contributed to the development of anti-Jewish doctrine:

- **Misreading of the New Testament** – Verses such as Matthew 21:43 ("the kingdom of God will be taken away from you and given to people producing its fruits") were read as divine rejection of all Jews, rather than as prophetic critique of leadership.

- **Flattening of Israel and the Church** – The unique callings of Israel and the Church were blurred. Instead of seeing Gentiles as grafted into Israel (Romans 11), they were seen as replacing Israel.

- **Allegorizing of Scripture** – Prophetic promises to Israel were reinterpreted as symbolic, applying only to the Church. The literal restoration of Israel was spiritualized.

- **Disregard for the Torah** – The Torah was portrayed as legalism, bondage, or a "dead letter," leading to contempt for Jewish observance.

These ideas were not peripheral—they became foundational to Western Christian theology.

The Messianic Jewish Response

Messianic Judaism challenges every aspect of supersessionism. It affirms that: God's covenant with Israel is eternal (Jeremiah 31:35–37).

- The Torah is holy, righteous, and good (Romans 7:12).

- Yeshua came not to abolish the Torah but to fulfill

it (Matthew 5:17).

- The gifts and calling of Israel are irrevocable (Romans 11:29).

Rather than replacing Israel, the *ekklesia* is invited into Israel's story. Gentiles are grafted into the olive tree, not a new tree (Romans 11:17–24). The nations join Israel, not displace her.

Messianic theologian Mark Kinzer describes this as "bilateral ecclesiology"—one body of Messiah composed of two distinct yet interdependent groups: Jews and Gentiles.[4] This model affirms Jewish identity and Torah faithfulness for Jews, while embracing Gentiles as full covenantal participants through Messiah.

Recovering the Olive Tree

Romans 11 presents a powerful corrective to anti-Jewish theology. Paul warns Gentile believers: "Do not boast against the branches. But if you do boast, it is not you who support the root but the root supports you" (Romans 11:18).

The metaphor of the olive tree affirms continuity between Israel and the *ekklesia*. The root is Israel's patriarchs and covenants. The branches are the Jewish people and believing Gentiles. The natural branches are not discarded but pruned for future restoration (Romans 11:23–24).

This vision is not only theological—it is eschatological. Paul writes: "For if their rejection leads to the reconciliation

---

[4] Mark S. Kinzer, *Postmissionary Messianic Judaism* (Brazos Press, 2005), 101–130.

of the world, what will their acceptance be but life from the dead?" (Romans 11:15).

The restoration of Israel is key to global redemption.

Hope for Reconciliation

In recent decades, many Christians have begun to repent of anti-Jewish theology. The Catholic Church's *Nostra Aetate*(1965) renounced the charge of deicide. Protestant theologians have re-examined their doctrines. Messianic Judaism has emerged as a prophetic movement, calling both Church and synagogue to deeper faithfulness.

The work of reconciliation is ongoing. It requires honesty about the past, theological humility, and mutual respect. As Paul wrote, "He Himself is our shalom, who made the two one" (Ephesians 2:14).

Conclusion: Turning from Error, Returning to the Root

Anti-Jewish theology was not an unfortunate misunderstanding—it was a deviation from God's covenantal plan. It cut the Church off from its own foundation, bore fruit in hatred, and obscured the gospel's Jewish heart.

Messianic Judaism calls for a return—not just to Jewish customs, but to a Jewish Messiah, a Jewish gospel, and a God who remains faithful to His people.

As we rediscover the olive tree, may we also rediscover the humility, love, and unity that defined the earliest followers of Yeshua. In their footsteps, we walk not in arrogance, but in awe.

<u>Reflection and Discussion Questions:</u>

- What are the historical roots of anti-Jewish theology in the Church?

- How has supersessionism affected Christian-Jewish relations over time?

- What is bilateral ecclesiology, and how does it correct the errors of replacement theology?

- In what ways does Romans 11 challenge the idea that the Church has replaced Israel?

- How can Messianic communities help build bridges between Christians and Jews today?

Chapter 13:
The Atoning Power of the Righteous – A Hidden Thread in Jewish and Messianic Thought

Among the most profound themes in both Jewish and Messianic theology is the idea that the suffering of the righteous can bring atonement to others. While traditional Christian theology centers the atoning work of Yeshua as a once-for-all sacrificial act, Jewish tradition also affirms that the merit—and suffering—of the righteous can have communal redemptive power. This chapter explores the theological bridge between these two streams of thought, showing that the notion of vicarious suffering and atonement is not foreign to Judaism, but deeply embedded within it.

Atonement in the Torah and Temple System

The Torah sets forth a sacrificial system that centers on the principle of substitution: the innocent animal bears the consequences of human sin. Leviticus 17:11 declares, "For the life of the flesh is in the blood, and I have given it to you on the altar to make atonement for your souls." The word for atonement, *kippur*, implies covering or reconciliation.

The *Yom Kippur* (Day of Atonement) rituals detailed in Leviticus 16 illustrate this vividly. The High Priest lays his hands upon a goat, confessing the sins of Israel before it is led into the wilderness, symbolically carrying away their iniquities. This act is corporate, priestly, and substitutionary.

Yet even in this sacrificial framework, the Torah hints

that sacrifices alone are insufficient. Hosea 6:6 declares, "For I delight in loyalty [mercy] and not sacrifice, knowledge of God more than burnt offerings." The prophets consistently call Israel to repentance and righteous living as the foundation for true atonement.

The Righteous as Substitutes in Jewish Tradition

One of the most compelling insights from rabbinic literature is the idea that the suffering of the righteous can provide atonement for others. The Talmud teaches: "The death of the righteous atones, just as the sacrifices atone" (b. Mo'ed Katan 28a).

Similarly, Midrash Genesis Rabbah 35:3 states: "The righteous are greater than the ministering angels... When they depart this world, they intercede for mercy on behalf of the generation."

The idea of the *tzaddik*, the righteous one, as a spiritual covering for the community is deeply ingrained in mystical and Hasidic thought. The *Zohar* (Vayikra 10a) teaches: "When the righteous pass away, they atone for the sins of the generation."

This notion does not replace Temple sacrifices but complements them. It affirms that the life and death of the righteous have cosmic significance.

Isaiah 53 and the Suffering Servant

Nowhere is this concept more central than in Isaiah 53. The "Suffering Servant" is described as one who "has borne our griefs," was "was pierced because of our transgressions," and "the chastisement for our *shalom* was upon Him, and by His stripes we are healed" (Isaiah 53:4–5). While traditional

Jewish interpretation has often understood the servant to represent Israel collectively, early rabbinic sources—including Targum Jonathan and Midrash Rabbah—apply this passage to a singular, righteous figure, even the Messiah.

Talmud Sanhedrin 98b refers to the Messiah as "the leper scholar," one who suffers for the sins of Israel. This aligns with Messianic interpretation, which sees Isaiah 53 as prophetically pointing to Yeshua's atoning death.

David Flusser, a Jewish scholar of early Christianity, noted: "The idea of the suffering Messiah is indeed Jewish… and was preserved in ancient Jewish texts."[1]

Yeshua as the Righteous Sufferer

In the *Besorah* (Gospels), Yeshua identifies with the *tzaddik* figure of Jewish expectation. He is portrayed as sinless, compassionate, and completely surrendered to God's will. His crucifixion is framed as a voluntary offering, not merely a Roman execution. Yeshua declares, "The Son of Man did not come to be served but to serve and to give His life as a ransom for many" (Mark 10:45).

His death is not a break with Jewish thought but its radical fulfillment. Hebrews 9:11–14 describes Yeshua as the heavenly High Priest, offering His own blood in the heavenly tabernacle to secure eternal redemption.

The early disciples saw His resurrection as divine vindication, confirming that His suffering was indeed redemptive—not only for Israel but for the nations.

---

[1] David Flusser, "The Suffering Messiah in Jewish Sources," *Immanuel* Journal 2 (1973): 37–44.

The Atoning Deaths of Martyrs

In later Jewish history, particularly after the destruction of the Temple, Jewish thought continued to affirm the redemptive nature of suffering. The deaths of the Ten Martyrs— rabbis executed by Rome—were seen as atoning acts.

The *Midrash Eleh Ezkerah,* read on *Yom Kippur,* recounts the martyrdom of Rabbi Akiva and others, portraying their deaths as "a sweet aroma before the Holy One." These stories shaped Jewish understanding of redemptive suffering.

In the *Shoah* (Holocaust), some Jewish thinkers even asked whether the millions who perished constituted a "sacrifice" for Israel. Though controversial, this reflects the persistent notion that innocent suffering can bear spiritual weight.

Messianic Implications

Messianic Judaism stands at the intersection of these streams. It affirms that Yeshua is the ultimate *tzaddik*, whose suffering fulfills and transcends all previous patterns. His death was not the rejection of Judaism but its climax—the Passover Lamb, the Suffering Servant, and the atoning Righteous One.

Mark Kinzer writes: "Yeshua's death should be seen not only as an atonement for sin but also as an act of priestly intercession on behalf of Israel and the nations."[2] Yeshua remains a Jewish figure, operating within Jewish categories, fulfilling Jewish expectations—yet with global consequences. His resurrection is not only personal triumph but communal promise.

---

[2] Mark S. Kinzer, *Postmissionary Messianic Judaism* (Brazos Press, 2005), 152– 160.

Reclaiming the Mystery

In modern theology, both Jewish and Christian, there is a temptation to rationalize or reduce atonement to legal formulas. But Scripture invites us into a mystery—a sacred drama of love, justice, mercy, and sacrifice.

A Messianic perspective holds this tension. We affirm substitution without simplification. We honor the Torah while receiving Yeshua's priestly role. We recognize that the righteous sufferer points to something larger than legal penalty: covenant restoration.

In this light, we can read Isaiah, the Talmud, and the Gospels as part of one unfolding story. The atoning power of the righteous is not only a doctrine—it is a testimony to the transforming love of God.

Reflection and Discussion Questions:

- How does the Jewish concept of the righteous sufferer enrich your understanding of Yeshua's atonement?

- In what ways does Isaiah 53 connect to both Jewish tradition and Messianic belief?

- Why is it important to understand Yeshua's death within a Jewish theological framework?

- How can modern believers embrace the mystery of atonement without oversimplifying it?

- What role does suffering play in spiritual leadership according to Scripture and Jewish thought?

Conclusion:
What Our Jewish Roots Mean for
Gentile Believers in Jesus

As we reach the end of this journey through the Jewish roots of our faith, it's natural to ask: So what? What difference does all of this make for me as a Gentile believer in Jesus? How does understanding the Jewish context of the gospel, the Torah, the feasts, and the people of Israel affect my spiritual journey with Yeshua? What is my place in God's unfolding story?

These are not just academic questions. They are deeply personal, shaping our identity, our worship, and our calling as followers of the Jewish Messiah. Let us reflect on what this means—practically, theologically, and spiritually—for every Gentile who confesses Jesus as Lord.

You Are Grafted In—Not a Guest, But Family

Paul's metaphor in Romans 11 is foundational: Gentile believers are "wild olive branches" grafted into the cultivated olive tree of Israel. This is not a secondary status or a mere invitation to observe from a distance. Rather, it is a declaration that, through faith in Messiah, Gentiles are full participants in the commonwealth of Israel, inheriting the promises, the covenants, and the hope that God first entrusted to the Jewish people.

This means your faith is not a new invention or a break from the past. It is a continuation of God's ancient plan—a plan that began with Abraham, was shaped at Sinai, and reached its climax in the life, death, and resurrection of

Yeshua. You are not a spiritual outsider. You are family, fully welcomed into the household of God.

The Old Testament Is Your Story, Too

For many Gentile Christians, the Hebrew Scriptures can feel distant or even obsolete. But as we have seen, the Old Testament is not just the prelude to the gospel; it is the foundation. Every story, every commandment, every festival points forward to Messiah and finds its fulfillment in Him.

When you read the Torah, the Psalms, or the Prophets, you are reading your own spiritual heritage. The Exodus is your story of redemption. The giving of the Torah is your invitation into covenant. The promises to Abraham, Isaac, and Jacob are, in Messiah, extended to you. The more you immerse yourself in this story, the deeper your faith will become.

The Jewishness of Jesus Deepens Your Discipleship

Understanding Jesus in His Jewish context transforms how we follow Him. Yeshua was not a generic spiritual teacher—He was a Jewish rabbi, the fulfillment of Israel's hope, and the living embodiment of Torah. His parables, miracles, and teachings are saturated with Jewish meaning and symbolism.

As a Gentile believer, learning about the Jewish roots of Jesus helps you hear His words as His first disciples did. It guards against misunderstanding and enriches your walk with Him. You begin to see the gospel not as a set of abstract doctrines, but as the outworking of God's covenant faithfulness to Israel and the nations.

Unity Without Uniformity: Honoring Distinctions

One of the most liberating truths of the Messianic perspective is that unity in Messiah does not require uniformity. The New Testament affirms a "one new man" (Ephesians 2:15), but it does not erase the distinction between Jew and Gentile. Rather, it celebrates diversity within unity.

Gentile believers are not called to become Jews, nor are Jews called to abandon their identity. Each has a unique role in God's redemptive plan. As a Gentile, you are invited to draw near, to learn, to participate—but not to appropriate or erase the distinct calling of Israel. This is a model of mutual respect, humility, and interdependence.

The Feasts and Rhythms of Israel: Invitation, Not Obligation

Many Gentile believers find great spiritual enrichment in celebrating the biblical feasts— *Pesach*, *Shavuot*, *Sukkot*, and more. These are not just "Jewish holidays"; they are God's appointed times, prophetic rehearsals of redemption, and windows into the heart of the gospel.

As a Gentile, you are welcome to participate in these rhythms—not as a matter of legalistic obligation, but as an act of worship and solidarity with the people of God. Observing the feasts can deepen your understanding of Jesus, connect you to the story of Israel, and foster unity with Jewish believers. But your righteousness before God is not based on these practices; it is rooted in faith in Messiah alone.

A Call to Stand with Israel and the Jewish People

To embrace your Jewish roots is also to stand against the

tragic history of anti-Jewish theology and supersessionism. For centuries, the Church taught that it had replaced Israel in God's plan, leading to misunderstanding, persecution, and loss. Messianic faith calls us to repentance and reconciliation.

As a Gentile believer, you are called to honor the ongoing covenant between God and Israel. This means rejecting replacement theology, opposing anti-Semitism in all its forms, and standing with the Jewish people—both those who believe in Yeshua and those who do not. It means praying for the peace of Jerusalem, supporting the restoration of Israel, and longing for the day when "all Israel will be saved" (Romans 11:26).

Living as a Covenant People—Together

The rediscovery of our Jewish roots calls us to a richer, more communal faith. In the biblical worldview, salvation is not just an individual experience; it is a calling to be part of a people—a covenant community shaped by God's Word, God's Spirit, and God's promises.

As a Gentile, your journey with Jesus is not a solitary path. You are part of a global family, joined to Jewish believers and to all who call on the name of the Lord. Your discipleship is lived out in community, in shared worship, in acts of justice and mercy, and in the rhythms of sacred time.

The Hope of the Messianic Kingdom

Finally, understanding your place in God's story fills your faith with hope. The prophets envisioned a day when all nations would stream to Jerusalem, when Torah would go forth from Zion, and when Messiah would reign in peace and justice. As a Gentile believer, you are a foretaste of that future—a sign that God's promises are being fulfilled, that the barriers are coming down, and that the kingdom is breaking in Your spiritual journey is not about escaping the world but about participating in its redemption. You are called to live as a citizen of the kingdom, to bear witness to the God of Israel, and to prepare for the day when every knee will bow and every tongue confess that Yeshua is Lord.

So What? Next Steps for Gentile Believers

- Embrace Your Identity in Messiah: Rejoice that you are grafted in, a full heir of the promises of God. Your faith is rooted in the story of Israel, fulfilled in Jesus.

- Deepen Your Engagement with Scripture: Read the Old Testament as your own spiritual heritage. Let the Torah, the Psalms, and the Prophets shape your understanding of God and Messiah.

- Learn from Jewish Tradition with Humility: Participate in the feasts, learn about Jewish customs, and honor the distinct calling of Israel. Do so as an act of worship, not as a means of earning righteousness.

- Stand Against Anti-Jewish Theologies: Reject any teaching that erases or replaces Israel. Stand in solidarity with the Jewish people, praying for their peace and salvation.

- Pursue Unity in Diversity: Celebrate the diversity of the Body of Messiah. Build relationships with Jewish believers, listen to their stories, and work together for the kingdom.

- Live as a Covenant Community: Practice your faith in community, not isolation. Join with others in worship, service, and the rhythms of sacred time.

- Anticipate the Coming Kingdom: Let your hope be shaped by the prophetic vision of Scripture. Live as a sign of the age to come, bearing witness to the God who keeps His promises.

Final Words:
Walking Forward Together

The rediscovery of our Jewish roots is not about nostalgia or legalism. It is about returning to the heart of the gospel—the good news that God has kept His covenant, that Messiah has come, and that all nations are invited to share in the blessings of Israel.

As a Gentile believer, you are not an outsider looking in. You are a beloved child of God, a fellow heir, a participant in the unfolding story of redemption. Your journey with Jesus is enriched, not diminished, by embracing the Jewish roots of your faith.

May you walk forward with humility, gratitude, and hope—rooted in the Scriptures, joined to the people of God, and filled with the Spirit of Messiah. May your life bear witness to the unity, diversity, and glory of the kingdom that is coming.

And may we, Jews and Gentiles together, hasten the day when the knowledge of the Lord will cover the earth as the waters cover the sea.

"And it will come to pass, that from one New Moon to another, and from one *Shabbat* to another, all flesh will come to bow down before Me," says *ADONAI*. (Isaiah 66:23)

Therefore, keep in mind that once you—Gentiles in the flesh—were called "uncircumcision" by those called "circumcision" (which is performed on flesh by hand). At that time you were separate from Messiah, excluded from the commonwealth of Israel and strangers to the covenants of promise, having no hope and without God in the world. But now in Messiah *Yeshua*, you who once were far off have been brought near by the blood of the Messiah" (Ephesians 2:11–13)

Let this be your story. Let this be your song. In Messiah, you are home.

For those who wish to go deeper into the Jewish roots of Christianity, Messianic Judaism, and the relationship between Jews and Gentiles in Messiah, the following books are highly recommended. These works represent a range of scholarly, theological, and practical perspectives, and are suitable for both newcomers and seasoned students.

Foundational Overviews

Understanding the Jewish Roots of Christianity: Biblical, Theological, and Historical Essays on the Relationship between Christianity and Judaism edited by Gerald R. McDermott.

A collection of essays by leading scholars that examines how Christianity emerged from Judaism, the ongoing relationship between the two, and the implications for theology and practice today.

A Handbook on the Jewish Roots of the Christian Faith edited by Craig A. Evans and David Mishkin.

A comprehensive yet concise primer covering the Old Testament background, Second Temple Judaism, the life of Jesus, the early Jewish followers of Jesus, and the ongoing interaction between Judaism and Christianity.

Our Father Abraham: Jewish Roots of the Christian Faith by Marvin R. Wilson.

A classic work that explores the Jewish foundations of Christian belief and practice, making a strong case for why Christians should understand and appreciate their Hebraic heritage.

Messianic Judaism: Identity and Practice

Messianic Judaism: A Modern Movement With an Ancient Past by David H. Stern

A clear and accessible introduction to the beliefs, practices, and history of Messianic Judaism, written by a pioneer in the movement and translator of the Complete Jewish Bible.

Introduction to Messianic Judaism: Its Ecclesial Context and Biblical Foundations edited by David Rudolph and Joel Willitts. An academic yet approachable overview of Messianic Judaism's theology, history, and its place within the wider Body of Messiah.

Voices of Messianic Judaism: Confronting Critical Issues Facing a Maturing Movement edited by Dan Juster

A collection of essays from various Messianic Jewish leaders addressing key theological and practical questions within the movement.

Jewish-Christian Relations and Theology

The Enduring Paradox: Exploratory Essays in Messianic Judaism by John Fischer

A thoughtful exploration of the theological and practical tensions in Messianic Judaism, especially regarding Jewish and Gentile identity in Messiah.

How Jewish Is Christianity? 2 Views on the Messianic Movement edited by Louis Goldberg

Presents different perspectives on the relationship between Christianity and Judaism, and the role of Messianic Judaism in bridging the two.

To the Jew First: The Case for Jewish Evangelism in Scripture and History by Darrell L. Bock and Mitch Glaser

Explores the biblical mandate and historical context for sharing the gospel with Jewish people.

Jesus in His Jewish Context

Matthew's Messiah: A Messianic Study of the Gospel of Matthew by Brandon Carpenter.

A passage-by-passage study of Matthew's gospel presented through a Second Temple period Jewish perspective. Complete with commentary and group discussion questions.

Mark's Messiah: A Messianic Study of the Gospel of Mark by Brandon Carpenter.

A passage-by-passage study of Mark's gospel presented through a Second Temple period Jewish perspective. Complete with commentary and group discussion questions.

Presenting the Messiah by Brandon Carpenter.

A study of various gospel narratives that are presented in a Second Temple period Jewish perspective. Complete with commentary and group discussion questions.

Reading the Bible with Rabbi Jesus: How a Jewish Perspective Can Transform Your Understanding by Lois Tverberg.

Offers practical insights into how understanding Jesus' Jewish context can enrich Bible study and discipleship.

Walking in the Dust of Rabbi Jesus: How the Jewish Words of Jesus Can Change Your Life by Lois Tverberg.

Explores the teachings of Jesus in their original Jewish context, making them come alive for modern readers.

Jesus and Judaism by E.P. Sanders.

A scholarly classic that situates Jesus firmly within the Judaism of His day, challenging many traditional assumptions.

Paul, the Early Church, and Jewish Law

Paul and Palestinian Judaism: A Comparison of Patterns of Religion by E.P. Sanders.

An influential study comparing Paul's theology with that of Second Temple Judaism.

The Partings of the Ways: Between Christianity and Judaism and Their Significance for the Character of Christianity by James D.G. Dunn.

Examines how and why Christianity and Judaism became distinct movements, and what this means for Christian identity.

Additional Recommendations

Israel Matters: Why Christians Must Think Differently about the People and the Land by Gerald R. McDermott.

A contemporary exploration of the theological and practical significance of Israel for Christians today.

Answering Jewish Objections to Jesus: New Testament Objections by Michael L. Brown.

A resource for understanding and responding to common Jewish objections to faith in Yeshua as Messiah.

Messiah in the Passover edited by Darrell L. Bock and Mitch Glaser. Explores the significance of Passover in both Jewish and Christian traditions, highlighting its fulfillment in Jesus.

Postmissionary Messianic Judaism by Mark Kinzer.

Explores how developing a distinct expression of Jewish life and faith in Yeshua can foster genuine Jewish-Christian dialogue and reshape the relationship between the Church and the Jewish people

These books will provide you with a solid foundation for further study, reflection, and growth as you continue to explore the richness of the Jewish roots of your faith in Jesus.

www.ingramcontent.com/pod-product-compliance
Lightning Source LLC
Chambersburg PA
CBHW070344130626
46556CB00007B/3024